LARRY RIVERS

For my wife, Maïa

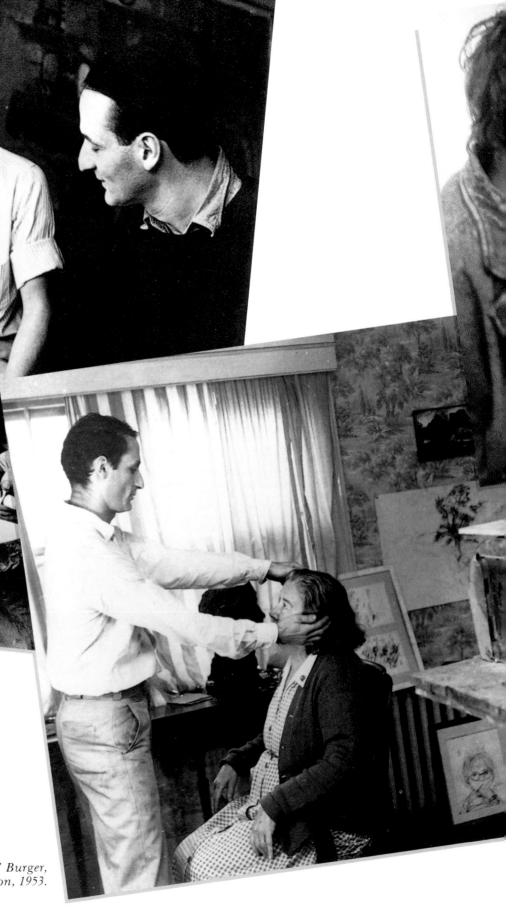

Larry Rivers with Frank O'Hara, working on the collaborative lithograph series.

The artist with his mother-in-law, "Berdie" Burger, Southampton, 1953.

Robert Rauschenberg, Henry
Geldzahler and Rivers,
New York, 1970.

The artist and his son Steven,
Southampton, 1954.

Rivers with
his daughters,
Emma and Gwynne,
Southampton, 1985

At the editorial offices of La Stampa, Turin, *with the painting,* Primo Levi: Witness, *1988, acquired by the Italian newspaper.*

Larry Rivers with his son Sam and Sam's mother, the painter Daria Deshuk.

In his Southampton studio, summer, 1985.

Daria Deshuk, the artist's longtime companion, with their son Sam.

LARRY RIVERS

BY SAM HUNTER

RIZZOLI
NEW YORK

I would like to express my appreciation to Larry Rivers, Daria Deshuk, Diana Molinari and Pat Malloy for the invaluable assistance they have rendered in assembling information and visual materials for this book. I am also most grateful to my ever-persisting and imperturbable secretary and assistant, Carolyn Bird, for her help in all phases of the manuscript preparation.

Flyleaf:
Larry Rivers playing his saxophone, 1960.

First published in 1989 by Rizzoli International Publications, Inc.
300 Park Avenue South, New York, NY 10010

Copyright ©1989 Ediciones Polígrafa, S.A.
All rights reserved. No part of this book may be reproduced in any form whatsoever without permission in writing from
Rizzoli International Publications, Inc.

Library of Congress Cataloging-in-Publication Data

Hunter, Sam. 1923
    Larry Rivers / Sam Hunter

     p.   cm
    Bibliography: p.
    1. Rivers, Larry, 1923-   —Criticism and interpretation.
I. Title.
N6537.R57H8   1989   89-50411
709.2—dc20   CIP
ISBN 0-8478-1094-1

Designed by Angelo Bucarelli

Printed and bound in Spain by La Polígrafa, S.A.
Parets del Vallès (Barcelona)
Dep. Leg. B. 27.940 - 1989

TABLE OF CONTENTS

10

Introduction

45

Larry Rivers, Public and Private

55

Notes

57

Color Plates

187

Black and White Plates

255

Drawings

341

Biography

343

One-Man Exhibitions

344

Public Collections

345

Plate Sections

INTRODUCTION

Over the past thirty years Larry Rivers has created a beguiling and original body of work of daunting multiplicity, and he continues to surprise even the most jaded tastes today by the freshness of his recent painted constructions on foamcore. His new synthesis of alternately painterly and constructivist strategies is still driven by his earliest impulses to intensify and make ever more palpable the illusionistic human image situated in space.

A list of Rivers' historical innovations is formidable. *Washington Crossing the Delaware* of 1953 was the first explicit effort by an American artist to assimilate popular folklore to the high style of advanced art, combining ghostly fragments of the grand manner with a devalued theme in a sensitive but, as we see now, relatively de-emphasized personal manner of handling and exposition. His multiple imagery, beginning in 1954 and 1955, became a mode of putting reality out of focus, and letting environmental trivia and banalities state themselves with a new and arresting vividness, far in advance of such methods and explorations as they were to take form in American Pop Art. The abstract expressionist cult of painting as a unique and unrepeatable experience was first, and grossly, compromised, by Rivers' shocking twin image variations on his nude mother-in-law in his *Double Portrait of Berdie*. The agile and digressive visual journalism that followed in his art can now be seen, in the light of succeeding practices, as a further deflation of the pictorial means as the exclusive carrier of content in painting, and it anticipated a general shift in contemporary esthetic motive and attitudes.

A study in depth of River' work over the past reveals a surprisingly coherent perspective amid the shifting variety of his style, even though his work does bridge, at times in giddy leaps, two distinct periods in American art, the subjective idealism of Action Painting and the new cult of literal experience. His art is at times full of strain and discontinuity, but it also brilliantly resolves and expands on its own contradictions, with a creative capacity large and generous. Stylistic contradiction suits his highly volatile personality and unpredictable shifts in mood and action. At the ripe age of 65, he is still a creature of impulse with a whim of iron.

Alertly tuned in on the present moment, he invokes the old masters. He may paint a free copy after Rembrandt's *Polish Rider* in a swift, direct manner and give his recycled cigarette brands the vintage look of a medieval emblem, each with an equivalent passion and in that spirit of open-mindedness which is one of his most appealing traits. From his earliest academies and studio nudes to his recent constructions in foamcore board relief, no matter in what register of expression from the elegant to the brute, his art is stamped with distinctive style and temperament. He has added something new and unforeseen to American art, at a time when the outlines and limits of originality seemed stabilized.

Yet Rivers came late to art, and by his own admission had the sort of childhood that was—to say the least—less than ideal for producing an artistic temperament. Born Yizroch Loiza Grossberg in the Bronx to Shiam (Sam) and Sonya (Shirley), Jewish Ukrainian immigrants, he began piano lessons at the age of seven so that he could accompany his plumber father when he played the violin. Around the age of eleven, the boy who by that time had changed his name to Irving, also changed his instrument—to the saxophone—and began a career in music.

While music was revered in the Grossberg home, the visual arts were not given a very high priority, Rivers has recalled with a certain tart clarity:

"The only things in our house resembling art were a cheap tapestry, a cross between a Fragonard and a Minsky popular in many dining rooms in the twenties, and a five-and-ten-cent store 8″ by 10″ reproduction of a Spanish señorita holding a flower just above an exposed breast, a painting which, to make matters worse, followed us from one apartment to another."

"Mind you, when I took my mother to her first exhibition of paintings—she having had such a profound dining room education in art—she told me which were good paintings and which were bad in a *very* strong voice. But if I've inherited natural bad taste, I'd praise my parents for passing on to me their strength, their natural physical endurance and animal concentration."[1]

That quality of innate, instinctive energy was useful to Rivers in his first artistic efforts, as he began playing the saxophone in his high school band and—by the age of 12—had begun to play professionally with jazz bands at Catskill resorts. It was at this time, in the early 1940's, that he changed his name to Larry Rivers after his group was introduced at a nightclub as "Larry Rivers and His Mudcats." Changing names was nothing new in his family. "My parents couldn't keep their names," he recalled. "Everyone called my mother something different. As a Jew she was called Sura. Her Russian name was Sonya, and when she came here, she was called Shirley. My father's name was Isaiah. It became the diminutive, Shiah, but everyone called him Sam."[2]

The taste for a variety of names came early and naturally for Rivers, but somehow leaving the Jewish element behind did cause him to examine his motives later, although he is well known for such works that emphasize his heritage as the vast historical pano-

rama and triptych which he mockingly entitled *History of Matzoh (The Story of the Jews)*. Long before painting his many works with overtly Jewish themes, Rivers found himself confronting the problem of Jewish identity, when he changed his name from Grossberg to Rivers. "So, that lies with me in my subconscious somewhere," he has said.

"My family always used to say, 'Well, why do you have to change—are you ashamed of Grossberg?' And I never would admit that. But in all probability it was whatever Jews go through with all those things—names and noses, and I had them all. I had all the bugs, all the neuroses. So later on I began to wonder if making paintings that have a Jewish theme was some way of proving that I'm not ashamed of it at all. I'm not. I'm very interested in the subject and prove it by devoting quite a few paintings to it."[3]

At the time of his name change, however, Rivers was far from showing any particular interest in art. In 1942, when he was 19 years old, the musician enlisted in the United States Army Air Corps, only to leave it with a medical discharge a year later. The official diagnosis of his mild, mysterious disease was multiple sclerosis, which never progressed, and when he left the corps in 1943, he took up his musical career again. The next year he began studying music at the Julliard School of Music in New York. Rivers also continued to tour as a musician and remained involved with the world of jazz and music.

About this time, several figures who would play a large part in Rivers' early development as an artist came into his life—oddly, through his music and through his marriage to a woman with a young son and a placid, passive mother. In 1945, he married Augusta Burger and became the father of her second son, Steven. Her mother, Berdie, was an easy-going, non-judgmental woman whose bulky presence dominated many of Rivers' key works until her death in 1957—and, in works such as his *Golden Oldies* series of 1979, long after her death. Unfortunately, the marriage between Rivers and Augusta was short-lived, and the couple separated in 1946.

In 1945, however, while playing at a resort in Old Orchard Beach, Maine, Rivers had met Jane Freilicher, a fledgling artist married to the band's pianist, and became for the first time interested in art. Impressed by her earnestness and intrigued by a world that was new to him, Rivers began sketching and discussing art with Freilicher. She encouraged him to paint, and introduced him to the complex and sophisticated modes of modern art in the form of Braque's cubist improvisation, *Homage to J.S. Bach,* which she considered closely linked to his background in music.

That summer Rivers began to paint seriously, making the transition from one art form to another smoothly. He rented a modest studio in New York on Twenty First Street, painting by day and playing saxophone by night. One of his neighbors, painter Nell Blaine, was the first established artist he met in the city; she was interested in jazz and included Freilicher and Rivers in her informal sketching class at her studio. Blaine had studied with Hans Hofmann and urged Rivers to enroll in Hofmann's studio, noting later "what impressed me in those days when he started...[was] that he worked so hard at it. The work was extremely naive, but it did have 'juice' of some kind."

"He never showed [those works]," Blaine recalled. "He painted white backgrounds and black lines like I was doing, and a bright yellow shape—pure colors."[4]

That naivete changed quickly once Rivers began studying with Hofmann, whose theories of "push and pull" seemed very natural to him, and shifted from jazz to art. "I began being less interested in that [jazz] world, and I began going to openings and things like that to do with art."

"But mainly now I'm beginning to go to shows, reading books, people are handing me things. Why is Cézanne so good? I don't see anything yet. It took me five years to realize that he must have something; everybody say he does. I did immediately see why the Old Masters were good...[and Hofmann] was talking about old art, he was talking about himself; I was deciphering that German accent and he talked about push and pull. He based everything on push and pull."

Hofmann was always making out that the size of the work, the rectangle, the square was the necessary ingredient in knowing why a work was successful, that within that space there was a certain amount of push and pull and the great geniuses understood that intuitively.

"So I said to him, 'Well, why do fragments interest us—we don't know the whole spatial setting?'" Rivers recalled. "In going to Hofmann, one of the things I suddenly realized is that he, like everyone else, had certain ideas and personal prejudices. By the time I got to him in the late forties he already was feeling his own oats as a successful artist... By the time I worked with him, he was feeling the breath of death on his neck, and he also was getting a reputation of some sort."[5]

At the end of the 1940s, Rivers, too, was acquiring a reputation. He continued to be involved to some extent with jazz, but was increasingly fascinated with art and artists of the past, particularly with the Impressionists and Post-Impressionists. In 1948, while taking classes at New York University under William Baziotes and other New York School luminaries with the goal of teaching art to support

himself, Rivers visited an exhibition of works by Pierre Bonnard at the Museum of Modern Art. Even in his classes with Hofmann, the arch abstractionist, he never left the figure behind.

Rivers always insisted on working representationally, Freilicher recalled. "Hofmann's thing was very spelled out. You were supposed to draw the figure and nothing else, actually, in a kind of abstract way, sort of sensing the planes. But Larry would interpolate his own themes and put a potted plant in the picture, or a rug on the floor, and make a little scene.

"Hofmann used to correct him and then, finally, Hofmann gave up and said, 'OK, Larry, you do it the way you want to.' Then he actually turned out some abstract painting, which were nice, and Hofmann was quite impressed with his talent, I think."[6]

Rivers' memory of his two years with Hofmann show his early sense of independence. "He gave up with me. He used to come out and talk like he didn't know me and then he used to say everybody has his distinctions and Larry does this kind of thing. Next. He didn't know how to deal with me, I thought.

"But he was very kind and very nice, and when I started having shows, and he would meet me on the street he would say, 'Congratulations, Larry, that was very good. You're dong fine and I really like the way things are going.' So he kept up an old-man-young-man thing and I appreciated it. You get something from school that the teacher doesn't even know you're getting."[7]

Gradually, during the late 1940s, Rivers turned from the frustrations of the jazz musician's life to the struggle to survive as an artist. It was a difficult time, and he has recalled it vividly in recent interviews and conversations. He was actively involved in making art, but had not left the world of jazz behind. "You don't just move into the future; you drag a past," he said. "I always had a little money—not much but more than most people I knew. So now you're getting to a point where I saw the Bonnard show and got a studio downtown on Madison Street and started painting.

"I used to run out of the house to get warm, it was so cold inside. I started painting very seriously there—it was a bare room and I'd set up a still life or whatever. Mostly it was chairs, or something like a Bonnard, with people sitting at a table. I'd worry about sex and women and cry to myself; I was a rather sad person then, and my sense of myself was that I was living a tragedy that I'm supposed to be a part of.

"I lived with it and it seemed to please me, my notion of myself. I took my instrument at night and went walking through the Village to find places to play."

While he was painting by day in his cold Madison Street studio and sitting in with various jazz bands by night—for free—Rivers' fascination with art continued to grow. He visited exhibits that inspired him, and spent time with other artists. To him, it was a new and heady experience.

"In the beginning I didn't really understand the modern French masters at all. Picasso was interesting because he seemed to represent something modern. Whatever it was, it looked like it must be good because everyone said it was good and it was so *peculiar*. But I didn't get it really. I started with Bonnard. I just began drawing the figure. I would ride with a pad on a bus. Everywhere I went I made quick sketches...I had done a paradise painting in 1948, all nudes, Bonnard nudes, about ten!

"These women were draped in casement windows—I was so far out of this world, I was dreaming up castles. Ingres' *Women in a Turkish Bath* may have had some influence on me, but I did it in a Bonnard style. Then I covered that painting with a painting of Christ kneeling in the garden, the moment before he was crucified. It was insane."[8]

In the spring of 1949, Rivers had his first solo exhibit, showing at the Jane Street Gallery 15 paintings inspired by Bonnard and the Impressionists, and by his everyday surroundings. At that time, he met the poet John Ashbery, who would become one of his closest friends and one of several poets with whose work he would identify, and he enjoyed favorable reviews by three noted critics—Clement Greenberg in the *Nation*, Elaine de Kooning in *Art News* and Stuart Preston in the *New York Times*.

At the high point of the collective creative surge of the New York School's abstract artists, Preston's remarks, however, paint a picture of the artist's work that is very different from the Rivers who would become famous for his sketchy, fragmentary, shocking canvases. The paintings "take no cognizance of the abstraction so prevalent in these last forty years," he wrote. "The great days of impressionism are evoked (one picture is actually, and properly, called *After Renoir*), for these big golden nudes, slowly undressing in sunny studios, riotous with the color of flowers, live in a joyous, decorative world."

Already Rivers was developing a mythic persona among his peers. Outgoing and theatrical, with a strong ego and powerful sense of mystery due partly to his chronic tremor, which might have become a fatal malady, but did not, and with his ongoing connections to the romantic world of jazz and drugs, the young artist clearly was on the path to a successful career. Nonetheless he agonized over his direction, and even when his work was selected for inclusion in the Talent 50 exhibit at the Kootz Gallery in New York by Clement Greenberg and Meyer Schapiro, his worries and crisis of confidence in himself did not abate.

Among other artists in the prestigious 1950 exhibit were Elaine de Kooning, Franz Kline, Alfred

Gustave Courbet: A Burial at Ornans, 1849
Oil on canvas, 124 x 263″, Musée d'Orsay, Louvre, Paris

I. **The Burial,** 1952, Oil on Canvas, 60 x 108"
Fort Wayne Art School and Museum Fort Wayne, Indiana

Leslie and Grace Hartigan—all rising stars in the New York art scene—but Rivers chose to abandon art temporarily in favor of writing. He gathered together enough money to go to Europe, spending several months in Paris before setting off for Italy.

While he was in Paris, he reevaluated his position as an artist. "Strangely enough, when I went to Paris in 1950 I was thinking to myself 'maybe I'm not an artist.' I sat around Paris and I wrote poetry the whole time I was there. I saw Paris and thought how beautiful-sad life is and how beautiful-sad my poems are and I didn't really do much painting," he recalled.

"I really did more living. I was twenty-six and I was just wondering what life was about. I went to museums, and I saw marvelous works in the Louvre. I went to a few shows. Going to Paris for me was going to the home of the Impressionists, the Cubists, the home of painting really. I think I suffered a few emotional setbacks in Paris. I met a girl or two, but nothing worked out as usual. So I stayed alone a lot in this apartment and wrote. I'd go out at night—I

probably was acting out some nineteenth-century idea of the artist searching for experience."[9]

Rivers may not have realized it at the time, but the experiences for which he was searching would have a lasting effect on his art. The impact of the works he saw—particularly the monumental history paintings displayed in the Louvre—was nothing less than overwhelming.

One particular work of supreme importance to Rivers was Gustav Courbet's monumental masterpiece of realism, *Burial at Ornans.* Measuring about ten by twenty-two feet, the 1849 canvas shocked viewers with its uncompromising, unremitting sense of the immediacy of death. Rivers was most impressed with the fact that the open grave was in the canvas' foreground, boldly proclaiming the fact of mortality to mourners and viewers alike.

It was at that time, in the early 1950s, that Rivers first began to synthesize history and his personal life. Just as the *Burial at Ornans,* with its mass of obscure persons jammed together in the gloom of black clothing and a dreary day, was of key significance to

Courbet, so the work that Rivers made after his trip to Europe, *The Burial*, held deep symbolic overtones for the modern artist.

While the composition and treatment of the 1951 canvas show Rivers' debt to Courbet, and its choppy brushwork and somber tones pay homage to de Kooning, Soutine and Bonnard, its inspiration was also very personal. "This is my grandmother's burial, actually, just as the *Burial at Ornans* was a personal experience of Courbet's,"[10] Rivers said of the expressionistic canvas, which measures five by nine feet.

"The thing about the *Burial at Ornans* is that Courbet actually put people whom he knew in it; he was also like one of those people that had double feelings about Paris—he felt he had to be there, and felt he was a country boy."[11]

Not long after completing *The Burial* and showing it at the Tibor de Nagy Gallery in New York, to mixed reviews, Rivers found the beginnings of a consistent and mature style. He would continue to blend grandiose historical themes with intense, often profoundly revealing personal narratives, and would continue to work in a representational, anecdotal manner that flew in the face of the period's dominant abstraction, much as he had during his classes at Hofmann's studio.

The earliest works to combine Rivers' characteristic style are a series of studies of his mother-in-law, Berdie Burger. In 1953, following a period of crises and illness, he took a house in Southampton with Berdie, his son Steven and stepson Joseph—his own version, perhaps, of Courbet's dual identity as a city and country boy. Between his return from Europe and his move to Southampton, Rivers had shown his work successfully, and his reputation had been solidly launched by the art dealer John Myers, who, Rivers said, "managed to get me money."[12] He extended his oeuvre to sculpture, modeling and then carving strangely commanding life-size figures in a mixture of plaster, cement and sand.

It was at this time that the pressures to support a family, separated though it was, and to maintain a "beat" lifestyle began to weigh heavily on Rivers. Myers described such alienating qualities in his life as "the distance, the skepticism, the refusal to be in one place, the denial of all middle-class values, even the (surrealistic) process of suspending consciousness to dredge up one's own resources." This sense of youthful vulnerability and alienation led to despondency and finally to an abortive suicide attempt on Rivers' part.[13]

After moving to Southampton, however, he concentrated on his work in his usual frenetic manner. "When my life took this romantically sad turn, I decided to get away from New York, and from New York's society," Rivers said. "I moved and rented a house for $85, and I supported myself by the sale of my work, by teaching once a week in the Great Neck adult education art program, and I had a private class. Also, I had a station wagon and I would truck people's furniture into New York. I supported myself that way until 1955."[14]

In Southampton Rivers had various odd jobs; he had a constant stream of visitors—and he had Berdie, his constant and faithful model. "She was a devoted creature. Berdie is the closest thing I've ever known to a saint. I don't mean that because I'm involved with saints. She had all the signs of being a little dense, but like saints are thought to be, she had no ego. She seemed to just be glad to be around and happy to be alive," Rivers recalled.

"She didn't have any relatives and she was just glad to be with me and the boys—and took care of them. She was very inept, she could hardly cook. She was nobody's idea of an old-fashioned mother-in-law in that sense. She tried, but she was just bad at it. But at the same time, she was very easy to be with... nothing upset her."

"I mean, here she was from a very ordinary Jewish background, born in Harlem when Harlem was still Jews. And there were gay guys in my life and black people and dope addicts and she would say, 'Oh, isn't he nice...and...he's nice...and...Tennessee Williams is nice.' She was slightly mad. A kind of glutton for punishment. The boys would walk all over her, and she'd just come back like the ocean. She was amazing."[15]

Equally amazing was the series of works that resulted from Rivers constantly sketching the complaisant Berdie in the garden in Southampton, as he tried to get one more drawing. His energetic renditions of Berdie were made during the period when he completed his groundbreaking painting *Washington Crossing the Delaware*, and although at first glance the portraits and the bombastic canvas could hardly seem more different, they express similar interests and are in the evanescent, fragmentary style that Rivers evolved during his Southampton years.

Washington Crossing the Delaware is in the tradition of the great history paintings that had impressed Rivers during his trip to Europe; yet it was created in response to a literary and not a visual work of art. In 1953, he was in Southampton reading *War and Peace* when he decided to create a monumental, modern work that had a patriotic theme. It was Rivers' way of declaring his artistic independence, of melding representation with abstraction in a subject so cliched that it would at once elicit amusement and become simply irrelevant.

"I wanted to make a work of art that included

II. **Washington Crossing the Delaware**, 1953, Oil on canvas, 83⅝ x 111⅛"
The Museum of Modern Art, New York, given anonymously

some aspects of national life, and so I chose Washington crossing the Delaware. It was like getting into the ring with Tolstoy,'' Rivers said. "The only thing was that Washington crossing the Delaware was always the dopiest, funniest thing in American life. Year after year, as a kid in school, you see these amateurish plays that are completely absurd but you know they represent patriotism—love of country, so here I am choosing something that everybody has this funny duality about.''

"It was also a way for me to just stick out my thumb at other people. I suddenly carved a little corner for myself. It seems to be something in my nature—I seem to fall on things that have a double edge... Luckily for me I didn't give a crap about what was going on at the time in New York painting. In fact, I was energetic and egomaniacal and, what is even more important, cocky and angry enough to

want to do something that no one in the New York art world could doubt was *disgusting, dead* and *absurd*. So what could be dopier than a painting dedicated to a national cliche?''[16]

The last artist to attempt the self-consciously noble, if entirely ludicrous, subject of a general crossing a river on a chilly day around Christmas with what Rivers called "hands-on-chest heroics" was Emmanuel Leutze, a nineteenth-century academic painter whose 1851 work includes classicizing, Napoleonic poses and beneficent beams of sunlight breaking through heavy clouds overhead, their forbidding nature echoed in the churning, icy river below. None of that neo-Baroque theatricality is present in Rivers' luminous version of the subject, which drew not from the Leutze painting but from what the artist refers to as "my own thing—I think History II."

"Certainly *Washington Crossing the Delaware* was the first attempt at really saying I'm an artist and I'm jumping into the ring," Rivers said. "I had to find my identity as an artist. In other words, can you believe I was an artist unless I did things that other artists did?"

"Things like that. I still do it, even though it sounds very, very—what's the word—philistine. Anybody can do abstract painting, I think somewhere I did think then that unless I really could draw like a Leonardo, I wasn't a *real* artist, a childish thing."

Inspired by this reading of Tolstoy more than by any desire to rebel or break away from accepted art forms, Rivers settled on a subject familiar to every American schoolchild and recast it in his new, impressionistic style.

"I read *War and Peace* for the first time and I was so moved by what I thought it was about—aside from the story and the drama, it was Tolstoy, a novelist, writing something. In other words, how could I as an artist equal something about that grand place that he presents for himself because of what he chose as his subject matter? I tried to find a kind of American equivalent, really. A very simplistic idea," he said.

"I tried to think of a work that would have that kind of general recognition to everybody and put some little thing that was personal on top of it, really...I think that most people didn't think that it was breaking away—they thought it was some kind of step backward or that it was like a conservative thing and really what it amounts to is that all these people, the Harold Rosenbergs and Clem Greenbergs or whoever, were so caught up in what they were doing that anyone who took a step that didn't seem to include their entire notion of what was important or interesting had to be thought of as some kind of reactionary or radical revolutionary."[17]

His goal in choosing Washington crossing the Delaware was far less complicated and political. The child of immigrants, he simply associated it with corny, sentimental plays that were performed on Friday nights in local school auditoriums. Thus his topic was both amusing and ridiculous, so familiar that it appeared invisible as a subject and could serve the same purpose as pure form in an abstract composition. Once he settled on its characters, on its episodic and somewhat cinematic format, he researched their costumes in the Southampton library, using a children's illustration book. He also drew from a lost Leonardo da Vinci cartoon of the Battle of Anghieri for the figure of a man with his mouth open, silently screaming orders.

Emanuel Leutze: Washington Crossing the Delaware, 1951
Oil on canvas, 149 x 255", The Metropolitan Museum of Art, New York

Such casual, apparently random methodology appealed to Rivers' sense of humor and appropriateness. He was aware that the Leutze work would seem to be the prototype for his painting, but saw no formal connection between the two. "The Leutze thing had nothing to do with me; my painting had to do with Tolstoy and the fact that I thought the subject was absurd and funny," he said. "And I did it in the year Joe McCarthy was at his height. I even have some letters somewhere saying that Joe McCarthy would take me as a patriot. I mean, the absurdity of history is that I might be seen as a kind of loyal, patriotic person although I took drugs and engaged in homosexual activities. In other words, what I was saying is that America as you know it wasn't true."[18]

When *Washington Crossing the Delaware* was shown, at the Tibor de Nagy Gallery in December 1953, the less-than-enthusiastic response did not surprise Rivers. "In the bar (the Cedar Tavern) where I could usually be found, a lot of painters laughed,"[19] he recalled. Nonetheless, within a short period of time many aspects of the Rivers' painting began to appear in the works of hs colleagues, including the sardonic stance and awareness of the importance of mass-media imagery that would lead to Pop Art within a few years. Despite the emphasis placed on Rivers' visual sources for *Washington Crossing the Delaware,* however, its deeper significance lay with such formal matters as paint application, arrangement of figures on the field and the blurring of various body parts and characters.

The soft, dispersed pictorial incident was concentrated by a boxlike frame made by Washington's boat in flattened, tilted perspective. Weak, painterly color tones contrast and blend with sketchy areas and superbly executed sketches that show through the thin overpainting like barely concealed *pentimenti,* allowing stronger forms to suddenly take shape. The overall effect is of strange, pulsating motion achieved by the interplay of forms and colors that keep the eye sweeping over the surface of the canvas, restlessly seeking a focal point and forever frustrated in that anticipated, irresistible effort.

Again, in his bringing together of historical—or established—painting and personal innovation, Rivers *is* very modern. As he recalled after seeing Gericault's *Officer of the Imperial Guard,* "It struck me suddenly that the passion in the picture is concentrated in a central passage—the officer and his rearing horse. That made me think that the important thing in painting is this sort of condensed passion, and I decided not to worry about borders, sidelines and accessories... If I can get the main impact right, I'm not concerned about surrounding details, and sometimes they weaken the principal image."[20]

Theodore Gericault: A Nude Study
Oil on canvas, 31¾ x 25⅜"
The Metropolitan Museum of Art, New York.

right:
III. **O'Hara,** 1954, Oil on canvas, 97 x 53"
Collection the artist

Rivers' intentions were again subjected to scrutiny—and the resultant controversy—during the next year, when he showed a number of academically "inspired" paintings of friends and family members, posed nude in a harsh and uncompromisingly naturalistic fashion. Chief among them were a study of Rivers' friend and collaborator, the poet Frank O'Hara, whose nudity is all the more shocking as it is contrasted with a pair of heavy shoes and socks, his former wife Augusta, who is presented as a sagging, unappealing Venus, and his gangling adolescent sons.

Most noteworthy, however, were Rivers' studies of the ever-patient, ever-present Berdie. Like so much of his work, the 1953 *Portrait of Berdie* is a hazy, half-felt and half-seen image that is more effective than a crisp, fully realized study would be. "These paintings consist of the faint remains of all the things that I did not want, that the whole canvas wouldn't give up no matter how I scrubbed, scraped or merged. So in a way, all of it grows out of an abundance of dissatisfactions,"[21] he said.

Indeed, the tension in Rivers' works of the early 1950s is reflected in his description of his method of working in the busy Southampton studio. "I drew everybody who came to see me. I had this idea that if you weren't drawing, working, painting, sculpting, doing some reading, something about art, you were wasting your time. All my twenties and thirties were lived in that kind of spirit. I mean, I was doing it all the time. I was a burden to a lot of people.

"I'm not your silent type and when I was drawing someone, I would talk about all sorts of subjects that had nothing to do with the drawing—but of course the people couldn't move. They could talk as much as they wanted except when I came to the mouth," he recalled. "Once I began, there was something so simple about getting the look of someone, doing it direct in pencil. There was no coloration, no orchestration, no question about 'what else is there going to be in my work? Where should I place it on the page?'

"My drawings were like moments."[22]

The Southampton phase of Rivers' career lasted until 1957, and the death of his chief model, Berdie. She sat for him in an old wicker chair, in an easy chair, standing and —most unforgettably—nude on the side of a bed. The intensity of the artist's observation in the 1954 pencil sketch, *Berdie Seated on Bed,* is more than matched in the fully realized oil painting from the next year, *Double Portrait of Berdie.*

They are the sort of works, excruciatingly observed and brilliantly realized, that led fellow artist Claes Oldenburg to comment on Rivers' working method. "He said, I seemed to continue beyond anybody's

The artist's mother-in-law, Mrs. Bertha ("Berdie") Burger, Southampton, 1953.

below:
IV. **Berdie Seated**
1953
Pencil on paper
8⅝ x 12"
Collection the artist

right:
V. **Portrait of Berdie**
1954
Oil on canvas
80¾ x 54⅜"
Museum of Art, Rhode Island School of Design Providence

point of belief," Rivers recalled. "I mean, I kept *at* something so long that it maybe finally becomes something. I don't know if it was a compliment or an insult—he was acting as if he really couldn't stand what I do, but you know, if I flatter myself into thinking that maybe I've done something, I just do keep at it."

"But I never think of myself as a person with patience at all; it's just that I want to get things so badly that I keep at it. I always think that I'd like to get something the first second I do it. The first second—I just want to get it all. And I don't. And then it becomes a matter of not being able to stand that anybody would see it bad."

"And so I'm undoing it, undoing it, correcting it, just to try to get it. It isn't out of some idea of perfection," Rivers said. "Why did I do so many pictures of [Berdie]. She was available—free. It wasn't that I felt like I was honoring her in some way. I'm very single-minded and selfish. She was just available and quiet. And I could do anything I wanted to do with her. I mean, since she had such underdeveloped vanity, I could never insult her by my work."[23]

In 1954, with the *Washington Crossing the Delaware* and his classicizing nude studies completed, Rivers felt he had already "gone through a whole period of that kind of painting—wiping, painting, wiping, charcoal" when suddenly he became bored

VI. **Double Portrait of Berdie,** 1955, Oil on canvas, 70¾ x 82½"
Whitney Museum of American Art, New York

VII. **Frank O'Hara with Hammer**
1955
Pencil on paper, 14 x 16½"
Collection the artist

VIII. **DeKooning with My Texas Hat**
1963
Pencil, crayon, cellophane tape on paper, 14 x 16⅞"
The Hirshhorn Museum and Sculpture Garden
Washington, D.C.

with the process and took a sudden new direction. He began to examine details that he had previously overlooked, and started to work with small brushes.

The precision of sections of the masterful *Double Portrait of Berdie,* the virtuoso passages of the shimmering flesh of her heavy breasts and the delicacy of the floral bedspread reflect his newfound interest, as do carefully rendered sketches on the wall behind the two versions of the artist's mother-in-law, one standing and one seated.

As in other works by Rivers, the viewer's attention is divided immediately between admiration for his technique and a slight, but definite, desire to avert the eyes before a model and theme so obviously not palatable. There is an awakening of the sense of prudery, and the viewer feels uncomfortably like a Peeping Tom in looking at Berdie's sagging flesh. Yet he soon suspects that the artist has chosen his theme for just that reason—to raise questions about what is and is not suitable subject matter, and indeed, what is beauty and truth to fact, and then to summarily dismiss the entire issue as pointless.

Seen in its context, then, as a work produced when such realism was completely outmoded, however acerbic and harsh it might be, *Double Portrait of Berdie* is a remarkable painting. The painting elicited an outcry from critic Leo Steinberg, who summarized it in *Arts* as "a picture in which genuine nastiness couples with false charm."[24] It was not just the starkness of the representation of an old, helpless woman that made the 1955 work so repellent; also seen as offensive were Rivers' lack of attention to such rudimentary aspects of anatomy as aligning the head and limbs convincingly, and his disjointed, fitful approach to his subject.

More serious was the response to the purportedly unimaginative and dispassionate repetition of the same form in the same format, as if Berdie were no more than another design element to be placed, lighted and depicted. In addition, by showing Berdie twice, Rivers took an unpopular stand against those who agreed with the Action painters' position that uniqueness was indispensable to expression. His use of background detail and the working of the surface also acted to subvert the gestural handling and spontaneity of Action Painting, even as its mood was echoed, imitated and parodied in some of the unfinished areas of *Double Portrait of Berdie.* Ironically, the painting was first seen publicly in the Ninth Street show at the Stable Gallery in 1955, the informal "independents" show organized annually at that time by the avant-garde and dominated by current abstract expressionist styles.

After the unrelenting, severe double study of Berdie, Rivers would never again be so harsh in his

IX. **Joseph,** 1954, Oil on canvas, 52½ x 45½″
Collection Frank M. Purnell, New York

vision. He followed the 1955 canvas with the softer, more lyrical *Berdie in the Garden,* the first of a number of similar studies of friends and family members. By the mid-fifties he had won a reputation as a gifted young portraitist, one of the few who could combine an interest in personality with a true personal style. Among the sketches made during this period are such striking portrayals of his close friend, Frank O'Hara, as *Two Blue Eyes, Frank O'Hara Seated, Hands Clasped* and *Frank O'Hara with Hammer.*

Just as moving are his penetrating sketches of poets Kenneth Koch and John Ashbery, artists Willem de Kooning and Grace Hartigan and a variety of friends, among them a sharp and shadowy study of critic Edwin Denby and the wispy, nearly invisible Molly Adams. In discussing the 1961 *Wiped Out, Portrait of Willem de Kooning,* one of many drawings of his friend, Rivers wrote, "Here he looks more vulnerable and you can see that I probably didn't like his nose."

"You know what that nose is composed of in the first drawing, and here I find that I must not have liked it, or not gotten it structurally satisfying, and so I tend to erase it, erase it, erase it, keep trying, erase, keep trying, erase, and finally in this case, I figured, well, let the observer make up more than I can represent. Sometimes a ·certain kind of paper won't give up a mark, so you just have the remains. This drawing is in the tradition of the kind of work in which the history of the work became part of its quality."[25]

More typical were portraits like those of his son *Joseph,* which fuses figure and a setting of a disorderly room with art books spilling from a bookcase, drawings tacked to the wall, a lamp close-up (these inanimate props were beginning to take on a mythic character, a convention of place identifying the stripped and essential outlines of the artist's world and his vocation). The nude melts into the environment, and as it does so, scattered touches of a free brush, smudges and decorative motifs assume added prominence. Although the realism is perfunctory, there are also fully realized details such as the model's socks which not only discordantly emphasize his nudity, but take on some further significance as the object of the artist's fascinated attention.

The increasing presence of the environment, with its intermittently perceived and banal detail—what Rivers rather prophetically called "common references"—at this early point is of particular interest, since his use of such elements preceded Pop Art by several years. From the mid- to the late-1950s, Rivers' depiction of these so-called "common references" increased steadily until such elements as Joseph's

bulky socks or the disembodied art books competed with Joseph himself for dominance as the work's true subject.

In addition, the use of commercial and stenciled lettering on the books made its first appearance at this point in Rivers' work—again serving as a foreshadowing of a key Pop Art motif. Nonetheless, he retained an essentially conservative format and remained committed to descriptive modes of figuration instead of shifting to an abstract or symbolic system of images.

In *The Family* Rivers posed his two undressed young sons with their fully clothed grandmother, in an obvious reference to Manet's *Déjeuner sur L'Herbe.* Like Manet, he enjoyed the contrast of textures of exposed flesh and the clothed figure, and complications of decorative motifs in the unfinished background. Another painting that brought notoriety, *Bedroom,* shows a married couple starkly nude, but their clear, unembarrassed regard and the increasingly deft, decorative pictorial accessories divert the eye from any prurient interest, as in the portrait of his son Joseph. It is Rivers' respect for his own experience, including an elementary candor about sex and gender, that emerges in these works, rather than a scandalous intention. And there is another quality which makes itself strongly felt: his mind's capacity for visual *non sequiturs* and significant distraction, psychologically so much like our perception of life itself as it is experienced.

This is the Stendhalian side of Rivers, the helpless inability to resist the *imprevu,* the unforeseen, and the ability to pass with curious impartiality from flesh to fabric, from highly charged aspects of reality in the human anatomy to the decorative surfaces of a room interior. The degree of his concentration on expanses of exhibited flesh almost seems to guarantee an equally intense, counterbalancing shift and fixation on decorative motif. Rivers later was to describe his art as "the smorgasbord of the recognizable." Such cunning digressions and snares for the eye take on an almost programmatic significance in his art. In this strategy was embedded the seed of a new aesthetic, for Rivers' permissiveness seemed to embrace a new way of seeing art and life, inviting them to operate freely on each other. Among the "academic ideas" which Jasper Johns some years later declared had influenced him was Rivers' sense of that lively interaction between the created and actual world. Johns refers to it as "the rotating point of view," and notes parenthetically, "Larry Rivers recently pointed to a black rectangle, two or three feet away from where he had been looking in a painting, and said '...like there's something happening over there too.'"

X. **The Twenty-Five Cent Summer Cap,** 1956, Oil on canvas, 53½ x 47″
The Hirshhorn Museum and Sculpture Garden, Washington, D.C.

In several mid-1950s works, among them *The Twenty-Five Cent Summer Cap, Berdie with the American Flag* and *Molly and Breakfast*, the mood Rivers had long admired in Bonnard and Renoir is recast in an abbreviated, nervous mode that is entirely contemporary in feeling—and entirely Rivers' own vision. *The Twenty-Five Cent Summer Cap* attaches the double image of the subject to his own trunk, as if two formerly distinct ideas could now be read as shifting aspects of a single reality. The main forms are sketchy and suggestive rather than full-bodied, loosely established in their larger outlines by an energetic code of dots and dashes, chained rectangles, and smears of greyed, vague color and flesh tints. So much flourish and small invention in linear detail give the images a stuttering, fragmentary legibility, but somehow life, movement and a sense of glowing physical well-being still do register, with great poetic charm. In all three works, figures are repeated in the same sort of double-exposure or time-lapse effect, creating a shifting, shimmering surface mobility, and the main figurative masses are sketchy, in contrast to the firmness of Berdie in her double portrait. Rivers' desire to involve the viewer in the process of creating the work, in completing the image-making by filling in the blanks and erasures, combines with his distrust of a finished surface.

His masterpiece of the period, *The Studio*, was painted in 1956 in Fairfield Porter's Southampton barn, using members of Rivers' circle of friends and family members. Its inspiration is another work by Courbet, this time the 1855 *The Painter's Studio*.

Rivers' monumental work—it is more than 16 feet long—is an airy, light-toned composition incorporating the characteristic repeated and evanescent figures of Joseph, Steven, Frank O'Hara and Berdie among such marginalia as the pot-bellied stove and the checkered pattern of Berdie's "evaporating" dress. The entire composition revolves around a primitivistic central figure, a surprisingly firm, dark-skinned dancer whose ritualistic gesture seems to be celebrating her nudity.

Far more than in the earlier works, the background has been dissolved and appears to be little more than an occasional grid of sketchy lines. Similarly, the players in Rivers' private drama have become ghostly notations, their motions recorded in a sort of stop-frame fashion that signals the passing of a swinging foot, say, or a head shifting to a more comfortable position. The sense of ease in Rivers' *The Studio* makes it an exceptionally graceful, elegiac heir to the weighty allegory and pomp of the Courbet of a century earlier; it is at once the Courbet's spiritual child and a pointed lesson in the meaning of modern art, emphasizing as it does the painted surface and the interplay of form and void.

Life, and Rivers' art, changed after 1957, the year of Berdie's death—and, oddly, the year he went on a popular network television game show, "The $64,000 Question," and won $32,000, with which he bought drinks for his friends at the legendary Cedar Tavern, preferred hangout and casual forum of ideas for the New York School artists since the late forties. Not surprisingly, the notoriety of the very public display

XI. **The Studio,** 1956, Oil on canvas, 82½ x 193½"
The Minneapolis Institute of Arts, Minneapolis, Minnesota

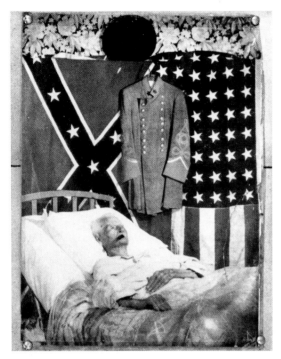

"Last Civil War Veteran," Life Magazine, May 11, 1959.

"End of the Gallant Rebs," photograph of Walter Williams, Life Magazine, January 11, posted in the artist's studio.

of his quick wit and retentive mind earned Rivers a rather unflattering profile in *Life* magazine as a "wonder boy" who could play jazz, paint masterpieces and win big all at once.

Rivers and his sons moved back into New York, and he began a series of works based on studio interiors, temporarily setting aside his interest in portraiture. It was at this time, in 1958 and 1959, that Rivers for the first time began to appear to resemble Action Painting in his work. His images were simplified and enlarged, and his surfaces were flooded with areas of homogeneous color in a manner reminiscent of Franz Kline in particular. The impressionistic lightness of the work of the mid-1950s was transformed into a far more solid, emphatic statement in powerful works such as the 1958 *Blue: The Byzantine Empress* and the almost completely abstract *Small Drugstore* and *Me In Rectangle,* two works from 1959.

The brooding, iconic quality of his post-Southampton works, which continued, nonetheless, to blend intimate personal history and an exterior, ready-made reality, was relieved somewhat in a series Rivers began in the early 1960s. Inspired by a January 11, 1960 *Life* magazine photograph of the last Civil War veteran lying in state with a Marine guard, "End of the Gallant Rebs," the artist once more found himself with an intriguing, macabre, patriotic and sentimental subject reminiscent of *Washington Crossing the Delaware.*

Rivers was tremendously intrigued with the subjects' narrative and visual potential. "It's sort of poignant, you know. The next to last Civil War veteran died—it was St. Patrick's Day, 1959, and he was a one-hundred-and-twelve year old man. About ten, fifteen years before his death, he was made into an honorary general and he used to sit on his porch in his uniform; people would pass by his house down in Tennessee, and they would salute him. I did a painting of him."

"Then once this 'next-to-the-last' confederate soldier died, there was this one guy left from the Civil War. Now he was a media thing immediately; the *last* Civil War veteran. So I began getting interested in *him* and I did paintings. Then he died. They started to look up his records and it turned out that maybe he lied—and the guy who was supposed to be the 'next-to-the-last' was actually the last. But this was covered up—and Mr. Walter Williams, I believe his name was, was buried with honors."

"This *Last Civil War Veteran* was done from a photograph that appeared in *Life* magazine of the vet in his coffin with a Marine guard. When it appeared, Ray Parker, the artist, sent it to me with a note reading 'Go!' He wanted me to do something with it, make a painting of it. He knew that somehow this had become a subject of mine."[26]

One large painting from the resultant series, *Dying and Dead Veteran*, combines two important aspects of the ceremonial photographs, presenting the duality of historical and present time in their depiction of the living and dead veterans. They also, significantly, incorporate the mass-circulation imagery with its anonymous registration of events that was of increasing interest to artists. The flag is a dominant image in all of the works in the series, expanding to fill a surface thaat is complex in its ornamentation and painterly in its technique. There are a number of large and small variations of this nostalgic theme, first in the sixties, and then repeated in a looser but more illustrative manner in the late seventies.

Equally gestural in style but more fragmentary and referential are such works from the period as the 1959 *Cedar Bar Menu I*, with its apparently random, fragmentary indications of setting and its crudely rendered list of entrees and prices, and the series of paintings and drawings based on a cigar box decal that includes the ironic, mocking *Webster Flowers* of 1961, the luminous, flat *Webster Superior* of the same year, and the more three-dimensional, sketchy *Electric Webster* of 1964. All contain the elements that also appeared in Pop Art, a style characterized by its cool, disengaged appropriation of slick images from everyday life, especially the advertising world. As the inventive bend of Action Painting headed towards standardization, and formal stereotype, the commonplace images of popular life and mass media gained in vivacity and interpretive potential for many artists. The drift toward a new kind of universalism of content, through the agency of the banal, actually began when de Kooning merged his symbols of private subjectivity with the immediate visual realities

XII. **Dying and Dead Veteran,** 1961, Oil on canvas, 70 x 94″
Private collection

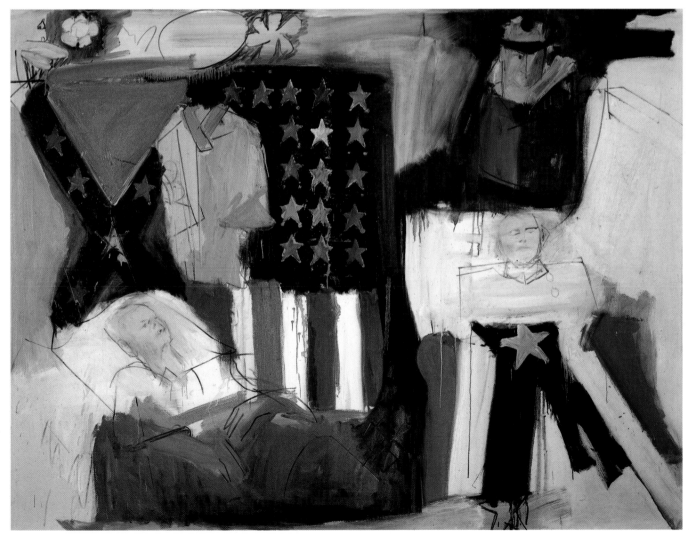

that lay at hand. He had started painting into his abstract spaces, in the early and late forties, indicatory signs for the outlines of his own fingers, written letters, matches in match folders and finally the overblown heroine of the billboards, Marilyn Monroe.

But in Rivers' hands, the emerging style is different from what became the conventional imagery and techniques of Pop Art. He had used such key Pop motifs as disembodied lettering years earlier, as part of the overall composition and not as the main subject. Rivers, however, monumentalized and transformed the graphic elements in familiar objects, treating them as vital parts of an expressive statement that is an intense record of reality. His responsiveness to visual stimulation, and his attachment to a per-

sonal, gestural style made the philosophical ambiguities felt in works by such Pop artists as Jasper Johns remote from his own intentions.

Rivers' personal life—and, by extension, his art—underwent a radical change in the early 1960s, when a Welsh girl named Clarice Price came to work as a maid and began to sit for him. "I did lots of drawings of her. She was an easy subject, willing to pose and quiet. She knew artists in England. By the time I got to know her, after she came to work for me in New York, she had posed for artists and she didn't seem to have an ego problem about it. Did it look like me? Did it make me good looking? Did it make me ugly?"

"She didn't have that at all. So she was a person that I drew a lot. Without thinking about it then, that

left:
XIII. **The Last Civil War Veteran,** 1960
Oil on board, 10 x 8″
Private collection

below:
XIV. **Buick Painting with P,** 1960, Oil on canvas, 48 x 61″
Collection Mr. and Mrs. Frank Titelman
Atlanta, Georgia

must have seemed an attractive quality for an artist who is interested in realism—not to worry about how the person is reacting... for a year, she was just someone who worked for me. She had a boyfriend, and I had Maxine... but it was sort of nice to see her there everyday and not be involved sexually—it always gets in the way. She was a happy sort of person, you know, she was nice. I got to know her better really that way, and then we got sexually close, and we were married."[27]

About that time, Rivers recalled, he was beginning to feel uncomfortable with naturalistic conventions. While still wanting to draw what he saw, he had begun to feel the need for some visual distraction in the work. "I wanted you to follow a limb, to see what somebody looked like, and at the same time I wanted you to begin to see that it is actually a drawing—it's about art; it is art."

"And so I began fitting rectangles around certain parts; I wanted to encase them. Later on Marisol carried this kind of thing further with her boxed-in figures, but this was much earlier, '62 or '63," he said. "Here's a [later] portrait of Clarice. It's pencil, crayon and airbrush on paper. And I'm using rectangles again, and here I've even sprayed a template. Again, I'm proving to my contemporaries that I'm arrogant about realism. I'm not that interested in it. My interests were varied."[28]

In his attempt to distract the viewer's eye, to call attention to the work as art and not reality itself, Rivers began to include stenciling in his paintings and drawings. Inspired by foreign-language books that instruct by showing, he placed crudely painted, childlike words next to a sensuous portrait of a casually posed, Rubenesque Clarice painted in 1962, *Parts of the Body—French.* He later included a few explicit labels beside her abdomen in an exaggerated nude, *Pregnancy Drawing* of 1964. He repeated the theme of the nude in a number of versions, large and small, with legends in a variety of foreign languages as well as English. The explicit inventory of the body's parts creates a curious split between perception and knowledge; we see the figure as an irreplaceable human subject, individual and whole, but we are also invited to read it through a screen of word-messages as a collection of replaceable or functional parts. Whether the mechanical lettering serves as a subterfuge for painterliness, or the painting act has become a mere ritual gesture, subordinate to elements of architectural design and structuring is difficult to decide; perhaps each and both are intended.

After 1961, popular and commercial images and insignia became a major element in Rivers' painting. He showed consistent if not immediately conscious preferences of subject in terms of his own particular

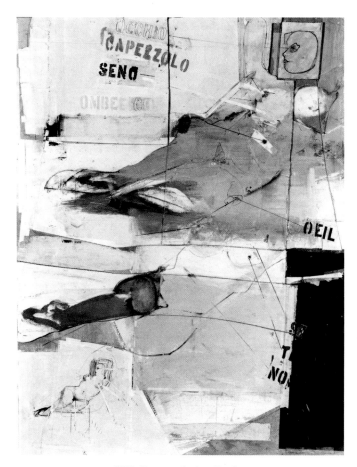

XV. **Parts of the Body**
(French and Italian Vocabulary), 1963
Oil and collage on board, 51½ x 40″
Collection the artist

attitudes and technical gifts. He was drawn to the Dutch Masters cigar box label because it in turn reproduced Rembrandt's *Syndics,* and gave him the opportunity to modulate a theme in both crude and more finished definition across popular media and back to its original source in fine art. The medium of traditional art is the theme of his popular subjects; the contemporary world, the object of his "fine art" handling and painterly virtuosity. The Daniel Webster cigar box cover oppresses the eye with its trite and primitivist icon, but the garlanded border invites the artist's free brush to operate expansively and thus subverts the image's impassivity.

While Pop-style paintings—cigar boxes and images with mechanical labels in Polish, Italian, French and even Persian superimposed on lush, painterly nudes—characterize the period of the early 1960s, they are not the only subjects that fascinated Rivers as he worked out his theories of art and its relation to life. Constantly toying with the notion that art is "half trickery," he drew from history throughout his career,

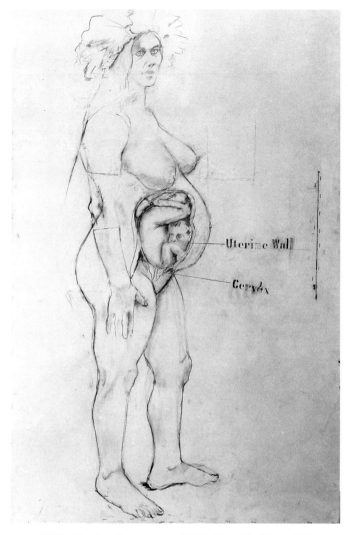

XVI. **Clarice Pregnant,** 1964, Pencil, 60 x 40″
Collection the artist

appealed to the fabulist side of his talent. Other sources in work of the sixties also explain themselves in terms of personal preferences; the ancient heraldic device of the modern playing card face; the Dreyfus Fund lions which stalk the street with a surrealist incongruity, but also mount pedestals to imitate public monuments, and besides tap a romantic vein of animal fantasy. All these images are cultivated assiduously as painterly occasions, and allude to their origins in the act of painting as well as to explicit popular sources and the special associations they may carry for the artist.

The iconic figure of Napoleon Bonaparte stands in full military garb in *The Greatest Homosexual,* one leg placed before the other and his hand inserted in his vest. Disconcertingly, insubstantial echoes of the main image indicate that he is not really here— this, after all, is not reality but art—and add eerie overtones that cause the viewer to examine a figure familiar from countless reproductions for some alternate, equally compelling meaning. As always, Rivers questions the nature of art and his subject in the works of *French Money* and *Greatest Homosexual* series in a way that seems calculated to disorient and to test his audience's tolerance.

Yet such divergent concerns as tenderness and overt eroticism also played a large part in his works of the period. *Lampman Loves It,* a sculpture made in 1966 of Plexiglas, painted wood and electric lights, contributed to his "bad-boy" status because of their unavoidably prurient overtones.

A cutout of a woman wearing only a shirt is shown bent over, exposing her posterior to the robot-like body of a black man captured in the act of penetrating her and who, raising the piece to new heights of outrageousness, has a readily recognizable visage. About such works Rivers' friend and fellow artist Howard Kanovitz once said, "He gets the smell of the bedroom in it."[29] Similarly, a 1969 mixed-media construction comparing a realistic dark-skinned penis and a pink one of equal size with a nine inch ruler, *America's Number One Problem,* is both witty and socially disturbing in its message.

Quite different in mood, though not in the willingness to experiment with mediums and styles and to blend the old and the new, is the 1967 mixed-media depiction of the Rivers family group, *The Elimination of Nostalgia* and *O'Hara Reading,* a print commemorating his dear friend, Frank O'Hara, the year after he was killed in a freak accident when a Jeep hit him on a Fire Island beach.

The mood in the group portrait should be one of cool detachment, yet the artist allows his feelings of compassion—not of the *de rigeur* cynicism implied by its saccharine subject and Pop style—to come

noting that no one knows how much work attributed to masters since the Renaissance was actually made by those masters and how much by studio assistants. His work, therefore, continued a long workshop tradition.

The melding of the historical, commercial and personal is particularly effective in two other series from this period, such works inspired by French currency as *Double French Money* and *Six French Money,* both from 1962, and a mincing series that pays tongue-in-cheek homage to the great classicizing painter of the French Revolution, David. Faces fade in and out of a rigidly organized, yet loosely painted format in the *French Money* paintings, their official nature undermined by the soft, soaked effects of Rivers' keynote "erasure" technique and made strangely intimate. The *French Money* series reincarnated Rivers' histrionic hero image, and the baroque ornament of the scrolled and foliated setting

XVII. **The Elimination of Nostalgia A, B, C,** 1967
Mixed media, 84 x 64½ x 25¾"
Collection Mr. and Mrs. Kent Klineman
New York

right:
XVIII. **Double French Money,** 1962
Oil on canvas, 72 x 60"
Collection Mr. and Mrs. Charles B. Benenson
Scarsdale, New York

through. Rivers was separated from his second wife, Clarice, and their two young daughters in 1967, and a sense of isolation, memory and, perhaps, regret color the three-dimensional *Elimination of Nostalgia.* "In the old days I remember thinking to myself that even the worst reasons can produce some good and interesting results," he recalled.

"A person may sit down and say he's going to write a poem because he wants to bother someone, and his motives may be completely unrelated to what finally appears. I did a painting called *The Elimination of Nostalgia,* as if doing the most nostalgic thing would get rid of it. It was a portrait of myself in leather boots, a very macho family man, my sons and my wife in a Victorian pose from a photograph.

"The title, *Elimination of Nostalgia* was to show that I had no interest in it. But actually it couldn't help but be nostalgic, and it is. As you're working, you really don't know what the end result of these things is going to be. Maybe what I was doing was what anthropologists call exorcising the spirits. I don't know. But it's always on my mind, I constantly think about it because I've been accused of dealing with nostalgia. And nostalgia—at least in the forties and fifties—was always deprecated. A high-brow type or an intellectual was supposed to separate himself from a folk interest."

"You were supposed to be ashamed of it. So it's been a conflict... It's like a problem with the superego," he mused. "You never can really decide what is leading you on, what are aesthetic considerations and what are ego concerns and commodity concerns. What is leading your hand? And the more you are aware of the dualities, ambiguities, contradictions in your character, the richer your work is, really. Only naive people think that what they do is pure and beautiful and full of... the *right* thing."[30]

At the same time, Rivers was profoundly affected by O'Hara's death. He read a heart-warming eulogy at the poet's memorial service, and produced several works specifically about him. Rivers also included him in such collage-like pieces as the somber 1967 *In Memory of the Dead,* which showed the poet at work, eyes downcast, while overhead floats the image of Berdie. "This is my morbid self, 1967," Rivers wrote about the work. "Frank had been dead about a year, and my mother-in-law for about ten years. I juxtaposed them both. This piece is a memorial to our collaboration. It seems as though Frank O'Hara has become some kind of culture figure, having died at the age that he did. His reputation far exceeds how he was regarded when he was alive."[31]

As the 1960s played out, Rivers' versatility in a variety of materials and media became more marked. Yet he continued to express his ongoing concerns for

XIX. **The History of the Russian Revolution: From Marx to Mayakovsky,** 1965
Mixed media construction, 53 pieces, 14'4" x 32'5" x 18"
The Hirshhorn Museum and Sculpture Garden Washington, D.C.

history and self, and to work with a variety of new mediums. Indeed, an inveterate experimentalism reemerged as the organizing principle of his artistic originality. In the face of the overwhelming transformation of art, his work submitted in influence to the changes it helped effect. Contrarily, the invasion of high art by the elementary modes of visualization and the pasteboard, emblematic reality of pop culture also impelled him to preserve, with added insistence, his own particular brand of individualism. He assimilated the Pop Art components of slick plastic, reproduced and mechanically transferred images, machine lettering and labels, and object appendages as choice morsels of felicitous handling. He used an actual window for the 1965 *Jim Dine Store Window,* so that he could change the artist's appearance by raising and lowering the sashes. He tried welding, carpentry, spray cans, airbrush and plastics, considering them all new toys that were especially enjoyable because the appeal of their novelty was also a part of his persona.

"I also think that I probably carry that out in my life, which is rather disturbing," Rivers said. "I mean, I think that I have that feeling with people, with bodies. At the same time, I could make a case for the opposite—that in my work at any rate there is some overall view or approach to subject matter that is there all the time. It's hard to know whether to give yourself a contemporary aura or to present yourself as some old master with all the perennial values."

In 1965, Rivers' various concerns with multimedia experiment, his compelling sense of history and of his own dramatic persona, as performer and hero, came together in his most ambitious and monumental collage construction, *The History of the Russian Revolution: From Marx to Mayakovsky.* The elaborate structure, assembled like a giant, narrative jigsaw puzzle of historical episodes and personalities, represented an extraordinary feat of individual effort, so much so that its personal expressiveness on such a grand scale took on, finally, a programmatic character. Rivers' expenditures of energy in execution focused attention once again on a kind of deliberately "solo" performance, and on an improvisational quality, painterly style, and slapdash construction that were clearly out of step with both the cool irony of Pop and the intellectual precision of Minimalism.

With its welter and vast spread of images, events from history, lettered signs, and object attachments, and its monumental size, the construction reads environmentally. It also gives the impression of stage flats, or scenery, because of the schematic nature of its description, and its clear definition and visibility at a great distance. The temporal sequence of images offers the most obvious structure and clue to the artist's intention, a "story" line that begins with a reference to the Revolution of 1848 and closes with an image of the poet Mayakovsky, a Luger at his head, the tragic suicide victim.

Accenting these and other images are such visual surprises as a boxlike section with real machine guns and rifles, which are played off against dummy rifles silhouetted in wood; a large map of Siberia traced over Plexiglas, with stenciled place names; linked rectangles of wood slats, which echo the color note of the unpainted dummy weapons and also abstractly summarize the basic structural motif of the work as a series of loosely connected rectilinear shapes. Yet the directional movement of paint crossing boundaries between separate panels provides transition and unity, conveying an ordered sense of the whole design.

When he had finished, Rivers declared the work "must be either a masterpiece, or an absurdity," obviously marvelling at the grandiosity of his project and its limitless pitfalls, as an epic if perhaps outmoded "history" painting in a "modern" style. Despite its flaws, eccentricities and obvious technical problems, the work is an extraordinary experience even today, twenty years after completion, for its expressive power, invention, and sustained intensity. It also represents a notable exercise of the contemporary historical imagination.

Rivers' use of the tremendous multiplicity of mediums that became available in the 1960s was coupled with his use of such drugs as amphetamines and, in the 1970s, cocaine. His earlier use of heroin had been closely linked to his jazz life, and during the 1960s Rivers had taken what he called "a fair amount of drugs."[32] He noted that he found them pleasurable, but not in any way conducive to making art.

"I didn't work under the influence of drugs. I didn't work 'high.' I couldn't. If I smoked pot, it would be social. If I took heroin, I would lie down. I never had a heroin habit, but I did take it from time to time," he recalled. "It was on speed that I did a lot of the three-dimensional works using new materials and carpentry. As I look back on it now, I have the same feeling that I have about the work of other periods when I didn't take speed—which is that some I like, and some I don't."[33]

Drugs, most notably psychedelic drugs, were a way of life in the 1960s and early 1970s, and whether the artists or advertisers actually took them, works such as Rivers' 1972 *Miss Popcorn* suggest altered states. Only the arms of the young model appear to be made of anything resembling flesh, and her solarized hair and reflective sunglasses give her the appearance of an insect or a creature from outer space—or a bad trip. Very much a part of its time, *Miss Popcorn* has a "cool, slick quality;" the artist noted. The work is airbrush on vinyl, and didn't fit in with "a certain notion people have about my work—or that I have myself," he said. "It changed

something in my art. It 'neatened me up.' The history or stages were no longer a part of it—I mean, how the work developed, my fingerprints and all that, went out of it."[34]

Gesture, however, is very much a part of recognizable Rivers works as the 1970 portrait of a young girl, *Snow Cap,* and the late 1960s *Africa* series, which was inspired by trips to the continent with filmmaker Pierre Gaisseau in 1967 and 1968. It also appears in his commissions for the New England Merchants National Bank in Boston, *The Boston Massacre* and *The Paul Revere Event,* and in the mid-1970s commission of overlapping images of a fashion model and wild African animals, *Beauty and Beasts.*

Larry Rivers' work since the seventies, particularly the masterful and widely divergent styles and subjects of the prolific past decade, suggests that he has reached a new level of complexity and has pushed his painting beyond the facile two-dimensional illusionism of his earlier oeuvre. The self-conscious, frequently playful references to Old Master paintings, which made their appearance some forty years ago in works that paraphrase Bonnard and Courbet continue to resurface in recent pastiches and parodies of masterpieces so well-known that Rivers' restatements inevitably seemed to take on an air of Pop Art, laced with his own highly personal irony. However, he has also embarked on new experiments in his recent relief constructions on foamcore boards that have given a dramatic and persuasive third dimension to his work without sacrificing its essential pictorial qualities or virtuoso skills in figuration.

Perhaps most notably at the close of the seventies, Rivers' long-held interest in texture, modeling and the abrupt interpolation of historical themes, both objective and subjective, once again made its distinctively personal appearance in his 1979 *Golden Oldies* series and in the *History of Matzoh (The Story of the Jews),* a monumental commission begun in 1982 and displayed at the Jewish Museum in New York in 1984.

Many of Rivers' familiar subjects reappeared in the two large canvases in the *Golden Oldies* series commissioned in 1977 by New York collector Jeffrey Loria on celebrating his fifties motifs, and the second, the sixties. Drawing on his own personal history much as he had drawn on the common bank of art historical imagery throughout his career, he recycled his 1960s imagery in the second painting, devoted to the sixties decade, recapitulating his familiar cigar-box design in *Portrait of Daniel Webster on a Flesh Field* and *Wide-Angled Webster* and his cigarette-box patterns in *Graph Camel* and *Two Camels.* A mincing Napoleon reappears in an acrylic-and-colored-pencil sketch, and the early 1960s

Vocabulary Lessons, in crisp, yet lushly rendered drawings. There are sketchy, characteristically fragmentary and wispy restatements of David's Napoleon as *The Greatest Homosexual* and also repeated cigarbox images drawn from Rembrandt's equally cliche *Syndics of the Drapery Guild,* which had been debased to the level of billboard advertisement. More significantly perhaps, the painting restates memorable tidbits from the treasury of iconic images that belong to Rivers' own past art. Multiple depictions of the camel on a cigarette pack overlap and intrude on sketches made in the Cézanne manner, and the *Language Lesson* features the face of his second wife, Clarice Price, floating above the grisaille recasting of the *Syndics* on the lid of the cigar box.

In the first recapitulation of his early themes, *Golden Oldies 50s,* a faded, blurred Washington, lifted from Rivers' 1953 canvas of *Washington Crossing the Delaware* and translated into a slightly more substantial demigod, poses below the firm sketches of the poet Frank O'Hara, who had died in 1966. A loosely printed list of daily fare at the Cedar Bar seems tacked high in one corner of the nervy, improvisational work much like a *trompe l'oeil* calling card detail in a work by William Harnett. The rich, jumbled images are jammed together in these immense canvases—they each measure 106 by 144 inches—as if in a randomly assembled scrapbook of great moments from the past, their variety, fresh juxtapositions and mood of real, if distant, nostalgia lending them a fresh, and unexpectedly moving, impact.

In 1982, Rivers began a commissioned work of staggering proportions, but one that held special interest for him. *History of Matzoh (The Story of the Jews)* presents 4000 years of history—always an irresistible topic—against a backdrop of an object so commonplace that it is iconic, the unleavened bread

XX. **Golden Oldies 60s,** 1978, Oil on canvas, 106 x 144″
Collection Sivia and Jeffrey H. Loria, New York

that the Jewish people carried with them when they fled into the desert in Biblical times. Each of the work's three panels measures 120 by 168 inches, and each deals with a specific period in the long, anguished story of Rivers' own ancestors.

In the complex typically collage-like and overlapping panels figures appear to move in and out of space, perceived only momentarily and peripherally because of their fragmentary, fading quality. Among the 24 distinct vignettes in Part I *(Before the Diaspora)* are an image of the fall of the walls of Jericho, derived from the work of early 20th-century artist Edmund Dulac, a rendering of David playing the harp, drawn from a 1915 work by American artist William Ladd Taylor and an idiosyncratic version of the familiar Michelangelo's *David,* here shown with markedly Semitic features.

The staccato, stuttering depiction of the 17 images in *Part II (European Jewry),* like those in *Part I* have been set against the lightly browned surface of the matzoh, as well as printed texts ranging from the spiky Hebrew of the tablets held aloft by Moses—for whom Rivers' cousin, Aaron Hochberg, posed—to an orante, illuminated *Song of Songs* and the 1401 decree in Cologne regulating the types of garments Jews were allowed to wear. The theme of suffering, repression and survival culminate in the portrait of Theodor Herzl, organizer of the Zionist movement that sought to establish a homeland for the Jews.

In the final part of the triptych, *Immigration to America,* a map of Europe is superimposed over the matzoh, and images of people moving humbly and quickly from steerage to sweatshop tell the story of the Jews from the late nineteenth century to World War I, when the largest waves of new Americans came from the Old World. As in Rivers' great history paintings, from *Washington Crossing the Delaware* to *The History of the Russian Revolution,* and such relatively ambitious efforts as the *Golden Oldies* and *Then and Now,* diverse pictorial elements overlap

XXI. **History of Matzoh** The Story of the Jews Part I, 1982 (detail)
Private collection

and fade into one another in *History of Matzoh*. Past and present, personal and impersonal elements are blended into seamless, fresh whole, and, depsite the seriousness of the work, a mood of energy and optimism predominates.

As the decades passed and the artist experimented with such widely divergent techniques and materials as airbrush and spray-painting, as well as incorporating plastics, carpentry and welding into his increasingly three-dimensional works, his interest in mixed-media construction continued to expand. In his work of the eighties Rivers has renewed his interest in translating two-dimensional paintings into palpable material form with his innovating foamcore sculpted relief structures. His complex technique of analytical dissection of pictorial fragments and their resynthesis as polychrome, painted relief gives a fresh actuality, a new conceptual rigor, to these three-dimensional constructions. He has now, in fact, created an elaborate workshop of skilled assistants and developed an entirely original procedure for converting his painted imagery into raised relief, utilizing an elaborate and time-consuming method of cutting up his painted surfaces into small and large segments, and then reassembling and translating them into sculpted constructions. The result is a highly intensified experience of a new kind of super-realism. His paintings have expanded into the third dimension, giving his figures an almost uncanny material presence, combined with more freedom in the invention of abstract shapes which serve both to contain and extend the painted imagery.

Rivers has always been a persistent experimenter with form and medium, and his recent restructuring impulse and surge of inventiveness recall his own past as much as they corroborate, and alertly echo, some of the collective artistic interests of the present moment. The artist has a happy faculty of constantly renewing his vision without imitating himself, and one great source of his originality has been a willingness to test the unities of his art unprejudiced by past achievement. Few artists paid less attention to conventional levels of tasteful finish and workmanship; yet few, for that matter, have matched his stylish refinements in draughtsmanship when the mood seized him. His mobile and restless interest in all manner of social and esthetic phenomena have perhaps given him a reputation for stylistic capriciousness, an inability to stay long within himself in a concentrated and sustained way. Yet it can be argued that the main source and object of his art are the unconfined play of the mind and eye, within that situation of multiplicity which he has so deeply grasped as one of the preemptive conditions of modern creation.

Around 1980, Rivers made the sort of digression into exotic subject matter that is so typical of his career, this time into the realm of the cultural and stylistic rather than—as in the 1960s and 1970s—into the blatantly historical, geographic or erotic. His excursion at that point was into the *Chinese Information—Travel* series, a collection of paintings and mixed-media pieces that range from the 1980 drawing-and-collage study of a jumble of horses and riders arranged decoratively across the surface of the paper, and the pale, ghostly grisaille painting that is closely related to it, *Chinese Information—Travel No. 1*.

The slightly later *Chinese Information: Female Rider* and *Chinese Information: Male Rider*, oil-on-canvas paintings on foamcore made between 1983 and 1986, continue Rivers' interest in the delicate, overlapping forms introduced in 1980. He made them more ornamental, however, by enlarging and exaggerating the central figures, giving them stronger tonalities and firmer textures and—perhaps most significantly—rendering them as low reliefs that cast shadows and project into our space. Yet the works are not so much sculptural as toylike, and their playful, decorative nature—combined with the lush, almost opaque painting—make them intriguing artistic asides.

Far more serious themes, directly related to the styles and subjects that have engaged Rivers throughout his career, are such portraits as the 1981 *From Photos of Gwynne and Emma Rivers*. The painting of family life is a more intimate and candid vision of personal experience, by contrast with the more public and historical themes anthologized in the two *Golden Oldies* paintings from the artist's past works. However, the painting also raises questions about the duality of sentimentality and prurience in his art, mainly owing to Rivers' inclusion of himself carefully painting the pubis of a scowling little girl who is his own daughter. In another 1981 painting from his tongue-in-cheek *The Continuing Interest in Abstract Art* series, *Then and Now*, Rivers portrays himself as a seated Rodinesque thinker in the middle of the canvas, flanked by Clarice on one side and her successor in his personal life placed at the right.

Rivers' "bad-boy" persona gained a little more notoriety that same year, with two acrylic paintings from that series, the somewhat leering *Sketches with Self-Portrait*, and the frankly naughty *Boucher's Punishment*. Even without a knowledge of art history, and of Boucher's role as the erotic painter of the rococo, the study of a Rivers-like figure seated on an upholstered chair about to strike the bare, rounded *derriere* of a gasping 1940s-style coquette could hardly be more titillating. The painting is remini-

XXII. **Public and Private** 1984-85, Oil on canvas, mounted on foamcore, 115 x 177"
Australian National Gallery, Canberra, Australia

scent of his matter-of-fact, yet somehow unsavory depiction of himself painting a child's private parts which also veers just a little beyond detached curiosity into perversity and questionable taste.

Rivers' ongoing fascination with historical narrative and the past was expanded and made more universal in *Public and Private* of 1985, a monumental acrylic-on-foamcore painting of such personal, deeply felt images as jazz players and reminiscences, once again, of Rivers' much-loved model and mother-in-law, Berdie Burger, and—by contrast—such cultural icons as a pompous General Eisenhower and a joyous, cavorting Fred Astaire. The dancer and his partners would appear repeatedly shortly after in a 1985 series that includes the three-dimensional, impressively animated *Dancer in an Abstract Field: Fred Twisting I* and *Dancer in an Abstract Field: Fred Flying I*, translating their kinetic energies into a modified form of static sculptural relief.

These syncopated studies are directly related to the more fully representational paintings of a year or two earlier with brilliant juxtapositions of stunning realism and blurred, out-of-focus passages. They are

mounted on sculpted foamcore to increase their sense of belonging at once to our world and to the world of art. Most notable are the romantic 1987 foamcore relief, *Make Believe Ballroom Dip* and the 1988 canvas-on-foamcore, *Dancer in an Abstract Field: Susan Bending.*

His extensive variations on the "dancer" theme was inspired in part by the kinetic experiments and the exercises in the dynamics of motion initiated historically by the Futurists and the English Vorticists. Indeed, the discovery of a 1913 watercolor by the English Vorticist, David Bomberg, confirmed for Rivers the relevance of his figure of Fred Astaire energetically levitating which he had already painted as a vignette in *Public and Private.* Bomberg may have suggested the mechanized and angular fragments that establish his planar structure so effectively in the later development of his fertile theme. His forms create a fascinating interplay between the real and the imaginary, in an ambiguous but logically conceived space that is both painted and sculpted. Areas that read as pigmented surface are continued, and expanded, by raised surfaces and solid shapes of

XXIII. A Vanished World: Trnava, Czecholsovakia, 1936 Raising Geese I, 1987
Oil on canvas, mounted on foamcore, 65½ x 60 x 5″
Private collection

an independent interest. Rivers seems concerned, with ever more insistent energy and urgency, to push his art today beyond the boundaries and limitations of the conventional medium of painting. A new *elan* in execution and the provocation of combining two- and three-dimensional figuration are evident in almost all of Rivers' current production. Among these are some of his most brash and decorative painting/sculpture syntheses: the 1983 *Cubism Today: Striped Face,* a lively, sculptural portrait of Roy Lichtenstein and his wife that is a brilliant hybrid sculpture relief and painting, and the 1986 *Work and Portrait of Red Grooms,* another illusionistic study of a contemporary artist and personal friend.

Equally memorable is the double portrait of the saxophonist and jazz musician, Sonny Simmons, who is shown in two positions, lying and standing before a bed as he plays his saxophone. The auto-biographical implications of this work seem obvious, especially since Rivers himself has wondered if he paints "...out of some overall interest in art, or... just a constant concern with myself as an artist—having been identified as an artist—and continuing that identity..."[35] The title is a pun which associates the sexuality of the Black musician with the art of music, specifically the Blues, and with the visual arts because of the stress placed on color. Further, it hints at a link between Rivers' self-perception and the powerful image which he has created. Rivers goes beyond autobiography in this work, however, dealing with the history and situation of Blacks in America and focusing, as he has in past work, on the way sexuality informs many of our attitudes and often stereotypical perceptions. Through subtle formal and rich painterly means, Rivers stresses the fact that this work is a fiction produced by the artist. The use of a double image, for example, and the way in which space is disjointed, produce a collage effect, as though one representation of the figure was cut from a pre-existing canvas and pasted onto another. Erasures also draw our attention to the surface of the canvas and the fictive status of painting as purely pictorial invention.

Nowhere are Rivers' extraordinary powers of formal and emotional synthesis more evident than in such recent works as the elegiac 1988 portrait, *Primo Levi: Periodic Table,* an oil painting of the holocaust author mounted on sculpted foamcore, as if to increase the image's poignancy by projecting it into the viewer's space. The scholarly and reflective Levi, late author of the deeply moving holocaust memoirs, sits calmly before two concentration camp ovens, their doors open and partly incinerated bones clearly visible within. Crudely printed words in harsh hues taken from the periodic table, symbolizing Levi's

Roman Vishniac, "Trnava, Czechoslovakia, 1936" from A Vanished World.

primary vocation as chemist, emphasize the horror and inhumanity of the camps, which Levi survived and about which he wrote so eloquently, while the brightness of the author's eyes and his quiet, conventional pose underline his consummate and refined sense of civilization. The exquisite finish of Levi's face stands in sharp contrast to the sketchy, more expressionistic brushwork of the ovens, and the almost provisional nature of his arms and shoulders, which appear to be mottled with fallen ashes.

The duality felt so strongly in the portrait of Levi is also present in the 1987 painted-canvas-on-sculpted-foamcore which just preceded the Levi portraits, *A Vanished World, Trnava, Czechoslovakia, 1936— Raising Geese.* In the initially lyrical study of a gaggle of geese in a farmyard, a bearded man whose features are faded as if in an old family album, gestures at the birds which walk away as if to symbolize the end of an era and recall, more specifically, the Nazi occupation, and the destruction of central European life and culture. The painting is based on a 1936 photograph by Roman Vishniac, and its deeply melancholy mood is very much in keeping with that of the Levi photograph, just as its appropriation of an iconic image and its translation into Rivers' keynote idiom is in keeping with the artist's constant concern for multiplicity, duality and candor about some of our most troubling emotions.

Clearly, many of Rivers' recent themes, the "dancer" series and even his somewhat more tender and touching studies of jazz musicians have been devoted primarily to light-hearted and hedonistic themes taken from the public world of the performance arts and entertainment.

Primo Levi, Turin, Italy, 1980

So repeated and common are these signposts and references that they suggest ego-identification and personal symbolism, or at least personal recollection. Yet, there is another more questioning and serious side to his recent art, linked more than once in the past to his awareness of his identity as a Jew and as a bohemian outsider. As he grows older, these themes are treated with a new depth of understanding and a compassion that defy the quite inadequate perception of Rivers as a merely gifted and arguably shallow entertainer, or as a man primarily of energy and sensual appetite. Another, deeper strain in his work is related perhaps to Joseph Conrads's "heart of darkness," a sense of the unspeakable and mysterious aspects of our destiny. It was hinted at in both Rivers' later historical paintings and his youthful studies of the "heroes" of his family circle and Bohemian entourage. Today these intimations of mortality have taken on a richer emotional color particularly in the intermittent revival of a subject matter of the holocaust and human suffering. Without presuming to reverse Rivers' preferred public image from hipster to moralizing preacher, one can legitimately point to an interesting new sobriety of tone in his art today, for an increasing portion of his creative and psychic energies seem committed to this new direction. There are signs of the birth of a richer vision of the conflicted self, moving Rivers towards themes of reconciliation and transcendence. A nascent but unmistakeable spiritual metaphor is present in his recent work, although the odd mingling of a clear-eyed pessimism and charity seems to run counter to his taste for the theatrical and self-projection in his early artistic production.

LARRY RIVERS, PUBLIC AND PRIVATE

Rivers has had a problematic relationship with his contemporaries and with cultural history from the beginning of his artistic career. Never one to resist a challenge or to conform, he often seemed to shift his style or approach just when his work was on the verge of acceptance, or to launch himself onto a difficult "new" and untried path when it appeared least advantageous.

Yet his inner sense of direction has made him one of the key innovators of his era, especially as a bridge between Abstract Expressionism and Pop Art. A realist who admired Bonnard and the Impressionists at a time when the lofty and ideologically rigid abstraction of the New York School dominated an art world newly centered in the metropolis, Rivers' hometown, he nonetheless maintained his position. By the mid-fifties, eight years before the debut of American Pop Art, he found a prophetic and pre-scient role himself with such works as the 1954 *Joseph,* a naturalistic portrait that included mass-produced, printed matter, and the iconic figurative cement sculptures of the same year that anticipate the style of George Segal's plaster molds of the human form in the sixties.

His first bold effort to challenge and change the direction of avant-garde taste was, of course, *Washington Crossing the Delaware.* Rivers patiently researched his project, but in an unexpected manner for the times, drawing impartially on popular and traditional sources. "I kept wanting to make a picture out of a national myth," Rivers told James Thrall Soby sometime later in an interview, "to accept the 'impossible' and the 'corny' as a challenge instead of running away... I guess I wanted to paint something in the tradition of the Salon picture, which modern artists hold in contempt."[36]

In its time, *Washington Crossing the Delaware* was cordially detested as a pastiche of historical styles, and a polemic directed at established avant-garde positions. The most controversial aspect of the painting was not its illusionism, or its surface charm, but the conscious decision to expend energy and sensibility on an outlived myth which the artist quite obviously knew to be trite to the point of meaninglessness. Before the era of Pop Art, or the theater of the absurd, one could not guess that the cliches which fall away from contemporary life or history as empty forms, could be revived as conventions in art because of their very ambiguity—their inane formality on the one hand, and the residual human or historical associations which still faintly echo in them.

Another strikingly anticipatory image drawn from his own inimitable repertory of private and public images was *Berdie with American Flag* of 1956.

Unlike Jasper Johns, who alienated the American flag from its public meanings and made it serve art in an enigmatic game of exchanged identities, Rivers did not try to confound the public and private esthetic meanings of his ensign. But he did use the flag, as he had used the subject of Washington's crossing, the old masters, and his real-life surroundings, because it was a simple fact that existed and did not have to be invented.

Nothing in Rivers' work before 1960 looks more contemporary even today than *The Accident* of 1957, for it presents a fresh vision of the agitated mosaic of urban life that has continued to stimulate our consciousness. The episodic and filmic action revolves around successive scenes of an auto accident on the New York streets; an injured victim is helped onto a stretcher and placed in an ambulance, detectives take notes, the life of the city goes on. Competitive with the depicted action are an intruding, lively jumble of realistic references to locale, printed legends in diminutive scale—the detail of a Hershey bar, detached from the side of a panel truck, the lettering "real" with estate obliterated—numbers, abstract signs in bright confetti colors, and fully painted passages in juicy impasto. The colliding realities of art and life coexist: an overturned vehicle sends up a spray of vaporous paint marks, a series of repeated circles become the wheels and movement of a car. The action of life and the medium of paint constantly interchange, and displace each other. Rivers builds a homely narrative, and its wealth of small, loving detail makes it seem like a Hans Christian Andersen fairy tale by comparison with the blunt shock-tactics and discontinuities of contemporary Pop Art.

XXIV. **Berdie with American Flag,** 1957, Oil on canvas, 20 x 25⅞″
The Nelson Gallery-Atkins Museum, Kansas City, Missouri

XXV. **Europe II,** 1956
Oil on canvas, 54 x 48″
Collection Mr. and Mrs. Donald Weisberger, New York

Warsaw, circa 1920. Source for
Europe II.

Perhaps sensing a growing diffuseness in his art and too great a graphic emphasis, in 1958 and 1959 Rivers for a brief interval began to take on the unequivocal look of an Action painter. He enlarged and simplified his images, and came under the influence of Franz Kline, flooding his surfaces with large homogenous areas of dark tone. The new turn in style was to culminate two years later in the painterly fullness and broad elisions of *Buick Painting with P* and *Ford Truck Painting,* works that state their message in simple powerful movements through meaty blocks of paint, without recourse to a more usual linear intricacy. Both of these potent images anticipate by two years the isolation of magnified signs and emblems of popular culture that were soon to dominate an important aspect of American imagist art.

The new breadth and simplification of manner were combined with a renewed interest in commonplace subject matter, alternating between the reproduced reality of the photograph and visual emblems of standard commercial brands. *Drugstore* is the first of a series of theme and variations based on an ancient photograph of the artist standing with a fresh-faced girl in a print dress before a pharmacy window which advertises Dr. West's miracle tuft brush. The photograph both as an intimate source of personal history and as a ready-made reduction of reality had attracted Rivers as early as 1956 in the painting he made of a family group, *Europe II.* First, family snapshots, and then special aspects of illustrated journalism offered Rivers a sense of continuity between his personal history and the movement of contemporary life, while putting the necessary distance between him and events. In *Drugstore,* and in subsequent themes taken from magazine photographs, he found a flatter, more iconic compositional form, without surrendering the quality of human sentiment that had always attracted him.

Two *Life* magazine photographs of the last surviving Civil War veteran, alive and lying in state, provided the kind of nostalgic and ceremonious occasion that particularly engaged Rivers' human sympathies and spurred pictorial invention. The manner of handling was not interpretive, and suggested neither melancholy nor regret, but the choice of episode was significant. Three large painted variations are based on the photograph of the ancient and feeble veteran among the living, two show his corpse laid out among his military relics and honors, and there are a number of wonderfully vivid small oil sketches on either theme; the large painting, *Dying and Dead Veteran,* combines both aspects. Their dualities include the sense of historical and present time, mass circulation imagery, with its anonymous registration of events, in the context of a personally inflected oil painting, and, of course, the two aspects of the human form, living and dead. In all versions the flag emblem is dominant and largely edits out the human presence, expanding to fill the flat surface of the painting.

In another line of development, Rivers' new work revolved around two of his principal iconographic preoccupations of many years, the Nude and the Hero. In Paris in 1961, he painted the head of his wife Clarice with sympathetic accuracy, labeling her features in strong block stenciled letters. He thus not only set up a contrast between fluid and mechanical draftsmanship, but on the level of information created a personal kind of literary-visual cubism that scrambled her features by naming them, even though the integrity of the image was not destroyed. He stumbled on the device of naming features and body parts in an elementary grammar book with visualized vocabulary drills, while studying French at the *Alliance Française* in Paris in the winter of 1961-62. The device of itemizing in standardized mechanical letters the parts of a complete and intact human image was subsequently applied to his wife's nude figure in such paintings as *Parts of the Body: French Lesson III*. He repeated the theme of the nude in a number of versions, large and small, with legends in a variety of foreign languages as well as English.

Whether the mechanical lettering served as a subterfuge for painterliness, or the painting act had become a mere ritual gesture, subordinate to elements of architectural design and structuring, was difficult to decide. Perhaps each and both were intended. Clearly, an increasing awareness of today's anonymous and efficient processing of products, which extends to cultural products, had an impact on Rivers' art in the sixties. But the impassive and flat expressive recipes of the commercial package, and popular art forms were inventively exploited. With the Parts of the Body theme, used images taken from correspondence course drawing manuals of the human figure, were torn apart and reassembled in dynamic formal arrangement. He then began to reconstruct them in plaster, mannequin figure groups, cast from actual display dummies and connected by obtrusive, raw geometric grids of iron; they retained the aspect of laborious manual effect in their rough-cut forms and inelegant surfaces, thus elucidating their own creative process of change and transformation.

By nature a questioning, demanding, impulsive character who pushed out to his own limits—and those of the people and institutions around him— Rivers nonetheless anticipated the cool, often sardonic art of the 1970s with his frenetic, uneasy jazz-and drug-influenced persona. He crossed over the line between the visual, literary and even performing arts in his personal and professional life again and again, seeking a synthesis in artistic media as he had done in his efforts to bring together high and low art forms, art history and personal mythology.

Works made in the gap between the visual and literary art forms include the lithograph from *Stones*, the 1958 collaboration with friend and poet Frank O'Hara, "To the entertainment of Patsy and Mike Goldberg," and, more recently, *A Song to the Avant-Garde*, a poem/painting piece by Kenneth Koch and Rivers that appeared in the November 1987 issue of *Artforum* magazine. In addition, Rivers' long-time habit of appropriating historical imagery and using traditional narrative motifs—however idiosyncratically expressed—have once again put him in the vanguard in recent years, this time as a postmodern master whose works range from the wittily outrageous 1981 study of himself about to paddle the bare behind of a voluptuous 1940s-style beauty, *The Continuing Interest in Abstract Art: Boucher's Punishment*, to the romantic, syncopated 1988 translations from cinema to shaped canvas of *Dancer on an Abstract Field: Fred Flying I*, and *Dancer on an Abstract Field: Susan Bending*.

Seen in retrospect, Rivers' astonishing and fertile career to date has been remarkable for more than its inventiveness, diversity and breadth of mood and vision. It also has been prophetic of the styles that would follow, as noted earlier. In his earliest years as an artist, after his 1949 show at the Jane Street Gallery in New York, when he moved to Southampton with his two sons and mother-in-law, Berdie, the restless Rivers hit upon his mature style, stimulated by reading Tolstoy's epic *War and Peace*. The result was unlike his earlier works, influenced as they were by Impressionist or Expressionist antecedents.

The vast, somber and elegiac 1953 canvas, *Washington Crossing the Delaware*, became virtually a catalog of everything Rivers would do for decades, from the stop-action or double-exposure presentation of figures, the blurring of edges and irrelevant areas, the willingness to work with a "corny" theme to the borrowing of the notion, if not the actual form, of various icons from the art of the past. In it, Rivers fused his taste for naturalism with an urge toward grandiose and even a self-mocking and pretentious repertory of gestures. But it seems clear today that he did so not simply to stand out, to be different from his fellow artist, but because he was expressing both his own deep needs, and touching a nerve in contemporary culture.

In those days a first, postwar generation of avant-

XXVI. From Public and Private: Fred Astaire, 1984
Pastel and pencil on paper, 20¼ x 27⅛"
Collection the artist

A source for From Public and Private: Fred Astaire.

garde giants bestrode the earth—especially in Greenwich Village. O'Hara recalled in a touching and revelatory 1965 memoir that there was "great respect for anything marvelous: when Larry introduced me to de Kooning I nearly got sick, as I almost did when I met Auden; if Jackson Pollock tore the door off the men's room at the Cedar it was something he did and was interesting, not an annoyance. You couldn't see into it anyway, and besides there was then a sense of genius. Or what Kline used to call 'the dream.'"

"Newman was at that time [the early 1950s] considered a temporarily silent oracle, being ill, Ad Reinhardt the most shrewd critic of the emergent 'art world,' Meyer Schapiro a god, and Alfred Barr was right up there alongside him but more distant, Holger Cahill another god but one who had abdicated to become more interested in 'the thing we're doing,' Clement Greenberg the discoverer, Harold Rosenberg the analyzer, and so on and so on..."

"Into this scene Larry came rather like a demented telephone. Nobody knew whether they wanted it in the library, the kitchen or the toilet, but it was electric. Nor did he. The single most important event in his artistic career was when de Kooning said his painting was like pressing your face into wet grass," O'Hara recalled. "From the whole jazz scene, which had gradually diminished to a mere recreation, Larry had emerged into the world of art with the sanction of one of his own gods, and indeed the only living one."[37]

Rivers' work, in a very real sense, is "a diary" of his personal and historical experience. "He is inspired directly by visual stimulation and his work is ambitious to save these experiences," said O'Hara, who knew him so intimately as a friend and fellow artist. "Where much of the art of our time has been involved with direct conceptual considerations, Rivers has chosen to mirror his preoccupations and enthusiasms in an unprogrammatic way."

"Rivers veers sharply, as if totally dependent on life impulses, until one observes an obsessively willful insistence on precisely what he is interested in. This goes for the father of our country as well as for the later Camel and Tareyton packs."

"Who, he seems to be saying, says they're corny? This is the opposite of pop art," O'Hara noted, in an important distinction. "He is never naive and never over-sophisticated."[38]

Rivers' interest in formulating a uniquely personal combination of his private life, including his musical activity, and the ever-present challenge of both contemporary art culture and the old masters continues in the eighties, which has become one of his most prolific and inventive decades. *Planned Parenthood*, the oil-on-canvas painting is mounted on foamcore, creates a powerful sculptural effect, showing his companion of the past seven years, Daria Deshuk, nude and pregnant, surrounded by images of mothers and babies and the lush, fertile flora of the tropics. With Rivers' irrestible impulse for truth-seeking, he presents symbolical depictions of menstrual blood and magnified sperms on the hectic journey upward to create new life. In the foreground of the complex, collage-like, sculptural painting is Rivers himself, his face enclosed in a blue box to emphasize the containment and concentration that characterize art, with his ever-ready saxophone in his hands. Just above his head floats an immense, erect dildo. The work is a joyous, hedonistic, almost primitive celebration of procreation, as process and fruition.

Less well known is Rivers' continuing interest in literature, and not just that of such poet-friends as Ashbery, Koch and O'Hara. The latter recalled in his famous memoir: "He has kept, sporadically, a fairly voluminous and definitely scandalous journal, has written some good poems of a diaristic (boosted by surrealism) nature... The separation of the arts, in the 'pure' sense, has never interested him."

"Larry is restless, impulsive and compulsive. He loves to work. I remember a typical moment in the late '50s when both Joan Mitchell and I were visiting the Hamptons and we were all lying on the beach, a state of relaxation Larry can never tolerate for long. Joan was wearing a particularly attractive boating hat and Larry insisted that they go back to his studio so he could make a drawing of her. It is a beautiful drawing, an interesting moment in our lives..."

"As Kenneth Koch once said of him, 'Larry has a floating subconscious—he's all intuition and no sense,'" O'Hara noted in his memoir.[39] Many have taken such remarks as derogatory, especially in relation to Rivers' paintings of the late fifties, finding his technique of description in this phase needlessly indirect and thin. In fact, a sense of ambiguity and complexity constantly enriches his style, then and now. He engages life aslant and impressionistically in his art, not head-on, extracting freshly observed truths from the visible world in small, successive shocks of delighted discovery that have finally a considerable cumulative density. The feeling for ideal human type is consistently sure, but under constant correction and amendment by its real-life reference.

His art brings together offsetting counterparts of form and personal gesture in a refined equilibrium. These double alternatives, sometimes parallel and often converging, are his art's major tension. His characteristic lightness of touch and virtuoso graphic gifts in themselves offer no certain test of his depth or richness of expression, as the sober sentiment of the works of the late eighties have made perfectly clear. To some extent his works may be seen as expressing a collective unconscious, the spirit of our time as much as the deliberate aims of the artist himself. And as such they are not the calculated efforts they may first seem, to rebel against the status quo, to carve a particular niche for himself or to find and create a market for his art, as a self-conscious program.

That they did so is coincidental, perhaps even miraculous, given Rivers' eccentricities and willful abandonment at certain points of the very work that was winning him most acclaim. In the 1950s, for example, on the heels of the successful reception of his work in an early exhibition, he went to Paris to become a poet. Fortunately, he was rather over-whelmed and intimidated by the size and grandeur of such great history paintings in the Louvre as Gustav Courbet's *Burial at Ornans*, and came home eager to paint again, seeking a new point of departure.

The groundbreaking *Washington Crossing the Delaware* of 1953, however, marked a sharp departure from the de Kooning and Soutine-influenced brush-work of his version of the Courbet masterwork in his painting *The Burial*. It was perceived by critics—and, indeed, by Rivers' friends and fellow artists—as a provocative call to arms, a deliberate attack on the serious and high-minded abstraction of the New York School. Rivers admired de Kooning, who also had worked with the figure and encouraged the younger artist, but Rivers chose to paint with thin, soaked washes in his first notable history painting, a bold departure from the gestural surfaces of de Kooning and his major expressionist influence, Soutine.

Today, however, Rivers himself, while admitting that the large history painting gave him a wonderful irresistible opportunity to thumb his nose at everyone, doesn't recall any particular desire to do that at the time, or to stake a new stylistic claim then outside of the de Kooning circle.

"I think that what my memory tells me—and that could even be faulted—but what would come closest to it would be that it wasn't so much that I was breaking away from everyone else, with *Washington Crossing the Delaware*. It's possible that I may have felt, what is all the hoopla about Jackson Pollock and all those people doing abstract art, you know, with no subject matter—just a lot of flurries and hand work, without any connection to art and life. It didn't leave me any room for myself. It's possible I had these thoughts, and also I did know a great deal about art history, about the gestures artists made in the past as they fought for their choices, and about

how you get out of the stage of history painting. I felt that if I took upon myself serious subjects, I would be taken seriously," Rivers recalled in a recent interview. "I still have that idea that I want to be serious, but at the same time that I cannot be serious without expressing some irony. There is always that dualism in my work. I am guided by these two feelings, serious and skeptical."[40]

That dichotomy, and the tension that results from the variety of other dualities that appear and reappear in Rivers' work during a span of almost four decades, made his work a potent call to arms in the early 1950s. They also played a seminal role in the later paintings of Rivers, and influenced the Pop practitioners who began using readily available mass-produced imagery in the sixties. Pop Art paralleled Rivers' art from the late fifties, beginning with *Cedar Bar Menu I,* 1959, to make more clearly ironist and even cynical social statements. The great difference between Rivers and the Pop artists who emerged in 1962, the year of the exhibition debuts in New York of Warhol, Lichtenstein, Dine, Rosenquist and others, was their nonchalance about ideas, whereas Rivers retained an old-generation commitment to the rhetoric of past ideology, and to art history and even social content of a sort. Rivers, however, never completely resolved the conflict between a quasi-expressionist technique and the commercial motif.

He was undoubtedly the first American artist to use so-called "vulgar", or vernacular subjects in a larger artistic context, but he did not take the idea to its extreme by simply recording his chosen imagery without comment or emotional coloring, as did Warhol, Lichtenstein, Rosenquist and others. His famous imagery of the sixties, the cigarette packs, Dutchmaster cigars, French Money, and the more wrenching Civil War Veteran series all retained certain emotional resonances, and he also masked their commercial derivation with refined painterly handling. Rivers in the late sixties, in fact, rather disdainfully denied any "super visual strength and mystery to the products of Mass Culture." He added, "I have a bad arm, and I am not interested in the art of holding up mirrors."[41]

Instead, he established a more complex subject matter as the basis of his art, although not necessarily its most critical aspect. In 1961 he listed four crucial elements: the choice and placement of color, its application and—tellingly—Life, the environment beyond the artist's control, noting that "only for the primitive and the semantically misinformed can enthusiasm for subject matter be the major inspiration for a painting."[42]

He noted that "life," an element that has nothing to do with critic Clement Greenberg's strictly formalist criteria for abstraction, is something like the digestive process. It is influenced by "everything but everything as it moves through the individual depositing mountainous amounts of material, adding and destroying and organizing on new bases as it passes through, creating associations, memory and passion and all those uncontrollable elements embodied in either yourself or the observer of a painting, that finally transform the obvious physical appearance into sensations and 'spiritual' significance." Simply stated, subject matter may play a key part in a work of art because it *is* life, Rivers wrote for a 1963 symposium on mass culture and the artist: "In order to paint I must look at something & I must think that in some way (the painting) is about the thing I'm looking at as well as the process of looking."[43]

Throughout his career he has been drawn alternately, and impartially, to the most casual aspects of ordinary existence and to the sacrosanct icons of the modern and old masters, to whose work, more often than not, he has given an irreverent and vernacular twist. He was also drawn to the human face and form and produced numerous individual and group portrait studies both of casual acquaintances, on commission, and of his own large circle of artistic and literary friends. Mainly, however, Rivers' art of nearly four decades offers the viewer the visual flow of everyday life. Most often the viewer is transported to the realm of Rivers' personal history, and to the pages of a family photo album, in such instances as the 1958 *Me II* and the 1979 *Wedding Photo (Social Patterns)*. The imagery here makes contact with Pop Art, but remains profoundly personal, if offhanded, in its associations and presentations. Alternately, there are the more direct painterly, often repeated depictions of cigarette packs, cigar boxes and other preferred commercial icons.

Rivers was captivated by mass-produced imagery, but only if they were of visual interest in their own right, thanks to their flatness and the "reduced conflict between what you are looking at and what you end up with on your canvas,"[44] he said. But it is likely that he also was drawn to their very ordinariness, to the fact that such objects are so omnipresent in our society that they become completely banal and unobtrusive. Unlike the overtly non-representational surface of a painting by Pollock or Kline, the equally hectic, gestural surface of a painting by Larry Rivers is the visual point of tension, not its representational subject. The subject is of so little appeal or interest, on occasion, that the viewer often dismisses it to focus more intently on the artist's composition and technique.

"I want to emphasize that this is a false choice

right:
XXVII. **Primo Levi (Double Head) II,** 1988
Oil on canvas, mounted on sculpted foamcore
73 x 58½ x 4″
Collection the artist

Concentration camp survivor, circa 1945.

XXVIII. **Wedding Photo (Apart)**, 1978-79
Pencil on paper, 29 x 36"
Collection the artist

between simple, homey interest in things, and worldly, *bad* overemphasis on surface and style," he said in *A Self-Portrait*, a radio lecture reprinted in the *Listener* in 1962. "Do not make it easy for yourself: not only doesn't the choice exist, you aren't even in a position to choose. And the other wide happy highway to visual glory, abstract painting, is still another over-simplification of choice. Better that we get rid of those dead bodies; perhaps we can resurrect something with a nastier, but more precise, quality of meat on it."[45]

Rivers' desire to get rid of the "dead bodies" and stereotypes of art was shared by many of his contemporaries, yet he himself seems never to have left anything behind or out of his widely inclusive paintings. The wealth of imagery in his works, from the Leonardesque sketches of flowers made in 1954 to the recycling of some of his favorite works—whether well-known or personal—in such paintings of the 1970s and early 1980s as *Golden Oldies 50s* and *Golden Oldies 60s*, and the elegiac *Public and Private*, from 1984, appears drawn eclectically from any and every possible source, a tendency O'Hara commented on more than two decades ago. Ironically, while in his early years he drew on such masterpieces as Courbet's *Burial at Ornans* and Rembrandt's *Syndics of the Drapery Guild*, he has been in the perhaps more self-conscious but also inevitable position of drawing upon himself more recently as a model and "old master."

That sense of involvement, of being part of history even as he looks back to it and mines it for imagery, makes Rivers' work very different today from such younger contemporary figurative artists as Mark Tansey and Michael Zwack who return reverently to the great art of the past for their styles, symbols and systems. Their attitude is less one of passionately embracing the vital force that inspired earlier works, however. Rather, it is a deconstructive approach, a detached appropriation of elements from civilization's vast collection of images, with their ready-made associations and recognition value. The orientation could hardly be further from Rivers' methodology and intentions.

When he created *Washington Crossing the Delaware*, Rivers was intrigued, as we have seen, by such obvious and available visual antecedents as the classicizing Emmanuel Leutze history painting, which presented what he considered in reality a cold and miserable human experience on an icy river as a glorious historical moment, complete with beatific beams of light bathing the heroic father of the new country standing steadfastly in the prow of a boat. Rivers, instead of drawing directly from the past to glorify an historic moment—and, by extension, bringing into play a wealth of associations engendered by the earlier work—as the postmodern painter might do, fragmented and gave contemporary meaning to the public theme in terms of his own artistic and personal concerns. Driven to create a grand historical panorama that might in some way affect the viewer as his reading of Tolstoy's *War and Peace* affected him, he researched Colonial costumes at the Southampton library, arranged his figures logically and dramatically on his large canvas and painted them with the thin, ghostly washes we know so well.

There is little borrowed glory in *Washington Crossing the Delaware,* as there is in works by the brilliant, gifted postmodern painters, and no desire to make glib statements about the values of a standardized, often dehumanizing society found in the Pop Art that drew liberally from Rivers' work. What, then, is the point of Rivers' habit of recycling such outworn patriotic myths as this one, and other related historical episodes and story-book fantasies, among them his "history" of the Russian Revolution and the idiosyncratic *History of Matzoh,* an epic of Jewish travail and achievement?

In Rivers' historical works the mood is serious but not solemn, tempered by irony and common sense, and most recently, in the Primo Levi portraiture and *A Vanished World* series, by compassion and tender reflection. These attitudes must be dissociated from the postmodernist complexities and the decon-

structive intentions of so much contemporary art. Rivers' approach to history remains essentially romantic and affirmative rather than cynical and disenchanted. He offers no radical critique of personal sentiment or historical allusion. His fictions and myths, public and private, emanate from a more trusting but also more stable structure of belief, whose values a new generation today ruthlessly questions and dismembers.

Rivers' paintings since the fifties make the important point, however, that new art and old, novel visions and tested truths from past traditions may coexist and even reinforce each other across the generation gap within a complex and constantly developing tradition. "New" does not *only* mean that which has been made recently, nor what is simply unlike anything seen before, since nearly every painting or sculpture is in some way different from all other. Nor are new insights and manifestations the exclusive prerogative of the young. It happens frequently that the artists who are the most original and influential at a particular moment are those who have been working for many years. Rivers' new painting is equally "of the moment," and remains a vital element in the ongoing complex dialogues and visual conversations between artists that shape new artistic traditions and advance the shared language of representational art today.

NOTES

[1] Larry Rivers with Carol Brightman, *Drawings and Digressions* (New York: Clarkson N. Potter, 1979), p. 25. A number of citations from the Brightman book have been revised by Rivers in conversation with the author on October 13, 1988.

[2] Ibid., p. 32.

[3] Ibid., pp. 29-30.

[4] Helen A. Harrison, *Larry Rivers* (New York: Harper & Row, 1984), p. 12.

[5] Interview with Sam Hunter, 1987.

[6] Harrison, p. 12.

[7] Hunter interview.

[8] Brightman, pp. 21-22.

[9] Ibid., p. 36.

[10] Hunter interview.

[11] Ibid.

[12] Brightman, p. 86.

[13] Harrison p. 21.

[14] Ibid., p. 25.

[15] Brightman, p. 51.

[16] Ibid., p. 59.

[17] Hunter interview.

[18] Ibid.

[19] Harrison, p. 37.

[20] Sam Hunter, *Larry Rivers* (New York: Harry N. Abrams, 1969), p. 25.

[21] Harrison, p. 38.

[22] Brightman, pp. 44-45.

[23] Ibid., p. 55.

[24] Hunter, *Larry Rivers,* p. 26.

[25] Brightman, p. 109.

[26] Ibid., p. 111.

[27] Ibid., p. 133.

[28] Ibid., pp. 133-135.

[29] Harrison, p. 79.

[30] Brightman, p. 176.

[31] Ibid., pp. 174-175.

[32] Ibid., p. 195.

[33] Ibid., pp. 195-196.

[34] Ibid., pp. 202-203.

[35] C. J. Everingham, "Symbolic Erasure: The Art of the Unknown Element," *The Houston Post,* September 9, 1984.

[36] Hunter, *Larry Rivers,* p. 24.

[37] Sam Hunter, *Larry Rivers* (Waltham, Massachusetts: Brandeis University exhibition catalogue, 1965), pp. 8-11.

[38] Ibid., p. 13.

[39] Ibid., p. 17.

[40] Hunter interview.

[41] Lucy L. Lippard, *Pop Art* (New York and Toronto: Oxford University Press, 1966), p. 78.

[42] Harrison, p. 46.

[43] Ibid., p. 46.

[44] Ibid., p. 48.

[45] Ibid., p. 48.

COLOR PLATES

1

1. **Studio Interior**
   1948
   Oil on paper, 17½ x 23½″
   Collection of Gloria and Dan Stern, New York

2. **Portrait of Frank O'Hara**
   1953
   Oil on canvas, 54 x 40″
   Collection the artist

2

3

3. **The Family**
1954-55
Oil on canvas, 82 x 72″
Collection Dr. Alvin Wesley, New York

4. **Augusta**
1954
Oil on canvas
83 x 53"
Collection
the artist

5

Europe

6

7

page 62
5. **Boy in Blue Denim** (Portrait of Steven)
   1955
   Oil on canvas, 53½ x 38″
   The Parrish Art Museum, Southampton, New York

page 63
6. **Europe I**
   1956
   Oil on canvas, 72 x 48″
   The Minneapolis Institute of Arts
   Anonymous gift

8

7. **The Journey**
1956
Oil on canvas, 104 x 115″
Collection the artist

8. **Molly and Breakfast**
1956
Oil on canvas, 48 x 72″
The Hirshhorn Museum and Sculpture Garden
Washington, D.C.

9

9. **The Accident**
1957
Oil on canvas, 84 x 90"
Collection Joseph E. Seagram & Sons, Inc.
New York

10

10. **The Pool**
1956
Oil, charcoal, and bronze paint on canvas, 8'7⅜" x 7'8⅝"
The Museum of Modern Art, New York.
Gift of Mr. & Mrs. Donald Weisberger

11

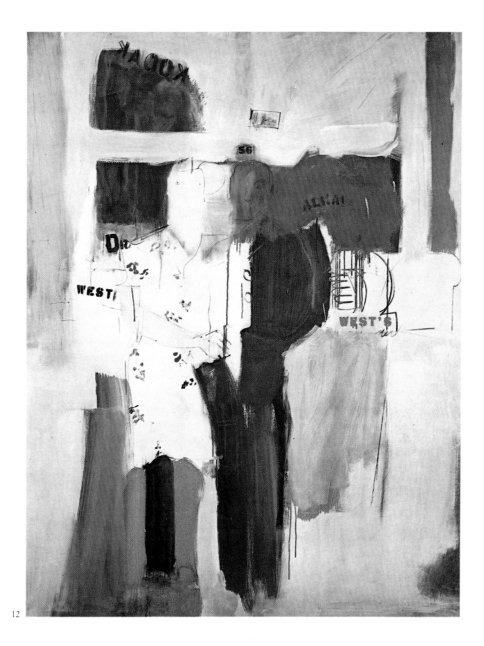

12

11. **It's Raining Anita Huffington**
    1957
    Oil on canvas, 104 x 115"
    Collection the artist

12. **Drugstore I**
    1959
    Oil on canvas, 85 x 66"
    Collection Mr. Barry Benedak
    Baltimore, Maryland

page 70
13. **Blue The Byzantine Empress**
    1958
    Oil on canvas, 72 x 60"
    Collection Mrs. Albert M. Greenfield
    Philadelphia, Pennsylvania

page 71
14. **Me in a Rectangle**
    1959
    Oil on canvas, 65¾ x 48¾"
    Neuberger Museum, State University of
    New York at Purchase
    Gift of Jane and Jay Braus

13

14

15

16

15. **Cedar Bar Menu I**
   1959
   Oil on canvas, 47½ x 35"
   Collection the artist

16. **U.N. Painting**
   1959
   Oil on canvas, 96 x 96"
   Marisa del Re Gallery, New York

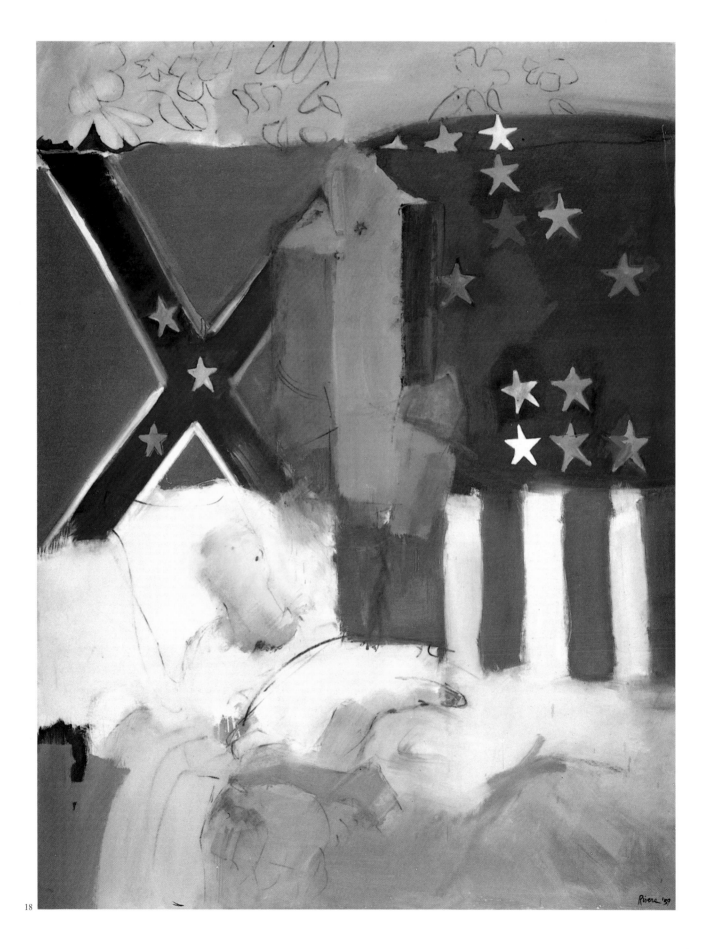

18

19

20

page 74
17. **The Next to Last Confederate**
1959
Oil on canvas, 60 x 46″
Collection Mr. and Mrs. Guy Weill
Scarsdale, New York

page 75
18. **The Last Civil War Veteran**
1959
Oil and charcoal on canvas, 82½ x 64½″
The Museum of Modern Art, New York
Blanchette Rockefeller Fund

19. **Final Veteran**
1960
Oil on canvas, 78¾ x 51″
Private collection

20. **Pink Tareyton**
1960
Oil on canvas, 12 x 9″
Collection the artist

21

22

21. **Pequeño as de espadas**
    1960
    Oil on canvas, 10 x 8″
    Collection the artist

22. **Kings**
    1960
    Oil on canvas, 52 x 60″
    Private collection

23

23. **Webster Flowers**
    1961
    Oil on canvas, 60 x 72"
    The Hirshhorn Museum and Sculpture Garden
    Washington, D.C.

24. **Barmitzvah Photograph Painting**
    1961
    Oil on canvas, 72 x 60"
    Collection George A.N. Schneider, New York

24

25

25. **Parts of the Face: French Vocabulary Lesson**
1961
Oil on canvas, 29½ x 29½″
The Tate Gallery, London

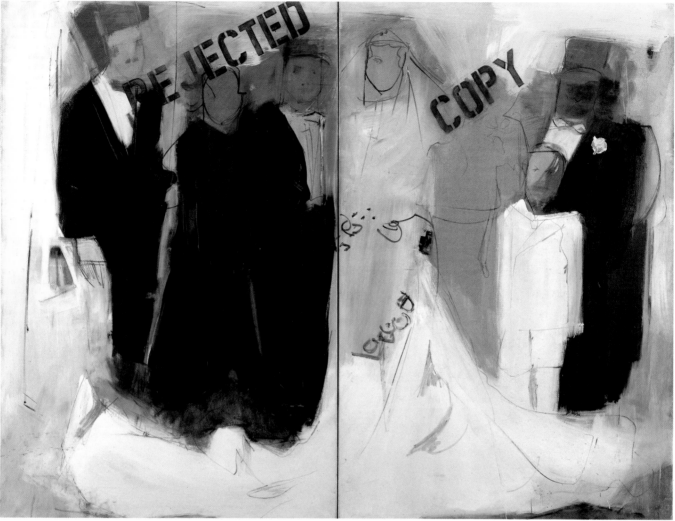

26

26. **Marriage Photograph**
1961
Oil on canvas, 71 x 98"
Private collection

27

27. **French Money Painting II**
    1962
    Oil and charcoal on linen, 35⅛ x 59″
    The Hirshhorn Museum and Sculpture Garden
    Washington, D.C.

28. **Italian Vocabulary Lesson**
    1962
    Oil on canvas, 30 x 24″
    Private collection

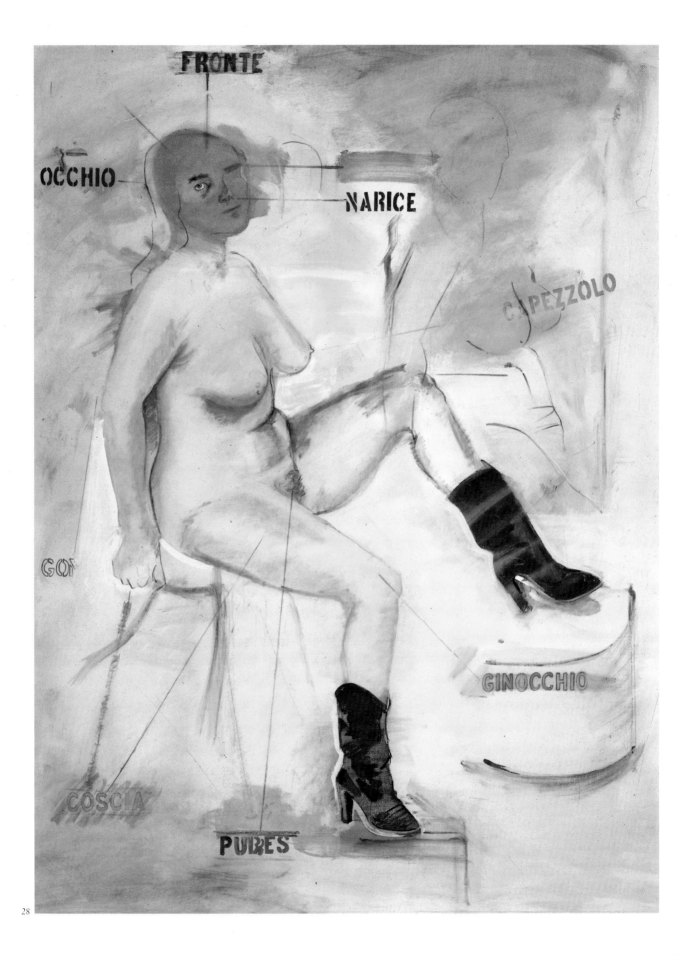

FRONTE

OCCHIO

NARICE

CAPEZZOLO

GO[...]

GINOCCHIO

COSCIA

PUBES

29

30

29. **Amel Camel**
    1962
    Oil on canvas and collage, 39 x 39″
    William College Museum of Art,
    Williamstown, Massachusetts

30. **Friendship of America and France**
    (Kennedy and DeGaulle)
    1961-62, repainted 1970
    Oil on canvas, 51½ x 76½″
    Private collection

page 88
31. **I Like Ingres—A Copy**
    1962
    Oil on canvas, 60 x 42″
    The Hirshhorn Museum and Sculpture Garden
    Washington, D.C.

page 89
32. **Portrait of Joseph H. Hirshhorn**
    1963
    Oil on canvas, 71 x 48″
    The Hirshhorn Museum and Sculpture Garden
    Washington, D.C.

31

32

33

33. **Celebrating Shakespeare's 400th Birthday**
(Titus Andronicus)
1963
Oil on canvas, 58 x 77¾″
Private collection

34

34. **Mauve Dutch Master**
1963
Oil and collage, 25 x 26″
Private collection

35

35. **Dutch Masters I**
1963
Oil on canvas, 40 x 50″
Collection The Fine Arts Center,
Cheekwood, Nashville, Tennessee

36. **Dutch Masters and Cigars II**
1963
Oil and board collage on canvas, 96 x 67⅜″
The Harry N. Abrams Family Collection, New York

36

37

94

38

37. **Camels 6 x 4**
    1962
    Oil on canvas, 72 x 48″
    Collection Mrs. J. Frederick Byers III, New York

38. **Africa II**
    1962-63
    Oil on canvas, 112¾ x 113″
    Collection Helyn and Ralph Goldenberg
    Chicago, Illinois

39

39. **Cézanne Stamp**
1963
Oil on canvas, 42 x 54″
The Hirshhorn Museum and Sculpture Garden
Washington, D.C.

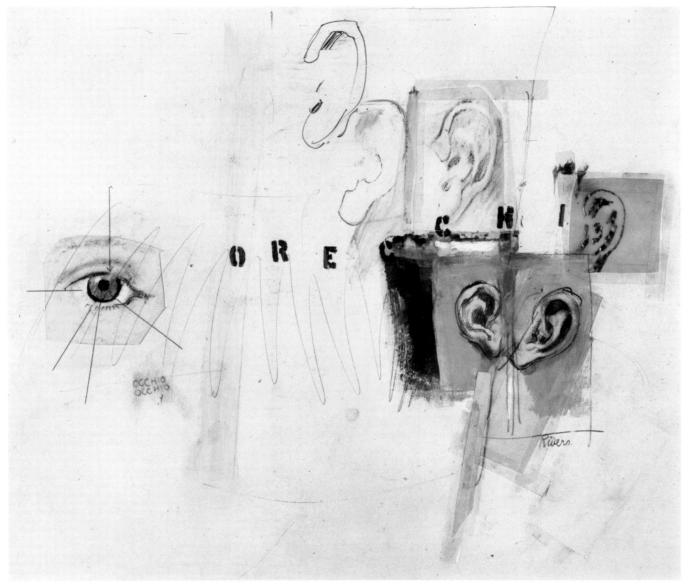

40

40. **Eyes and Ears**
    1963
    Oil, pencil and paper collage on paper, 14¾ x 18″
    Private collection

41

42

41. **Parts of the Body: English Vocabulary Lesson**
    1963
    Oil and collage on board, 60 x 40″
    Richard Gray Gallery, Chicago

42. **Lions on the Dreyfus Fund III**
    1964
    Oil and collage with stencil cutouts on canvas, 14½ x 78½″
    The Art Institute of Chicago, Illinois

43

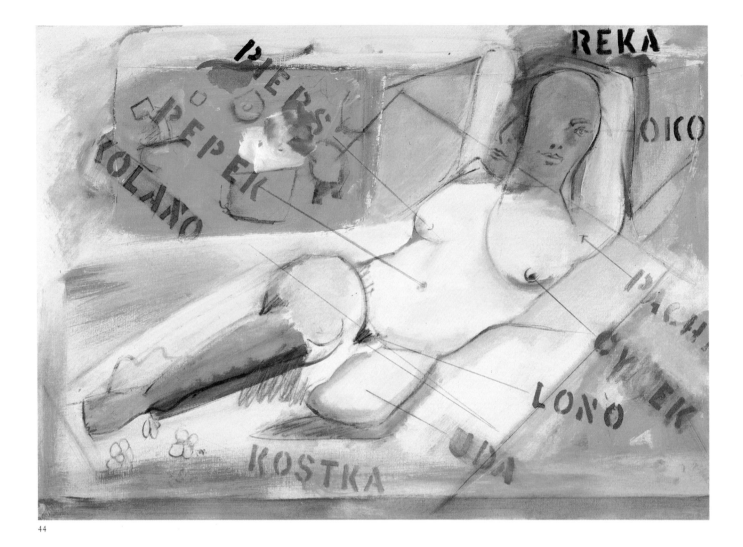

44

43. **The Greatest Homosexual**
    1964
    Oil and collage on canvas, 80 x 61"
    The Hirshhorn Museum and Sculpture Garden
    Washington, D.C.

44. **Polish Vocabulary Lesson**
    1964
    Oil on canvas, 24 x 30"
    Private collection

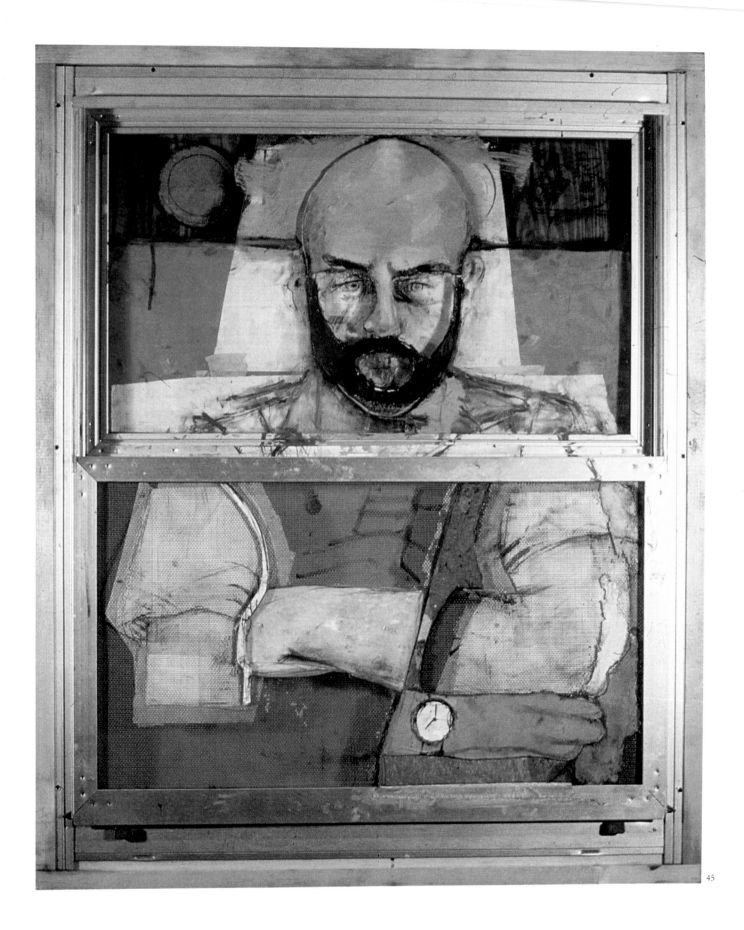

46

45. **Jim Dine Storm Windows**
1965
Mixed media, 29 x 25 x 2¾″
Collection the artist

46. **Plexiglas Playmate**
1966
Mixed media, 62 x 49 x 15″
Collection Playboy Club
Chicago, Illinois

47

47. **Webster and Europe**
1967
Relief collage with crayon and charcoal, 18 x 20″
The Phoenix Art Museum, Phoenix, Arizona
(Gift of Mr. Edward Jacobson)

48

48. **The Boston Massacre** (detail)
1968
Acrylic and oil on canvas, 19'6" x 14" (full size)
Collection The New England Merchants National
Bank of Boston, Massachusetts

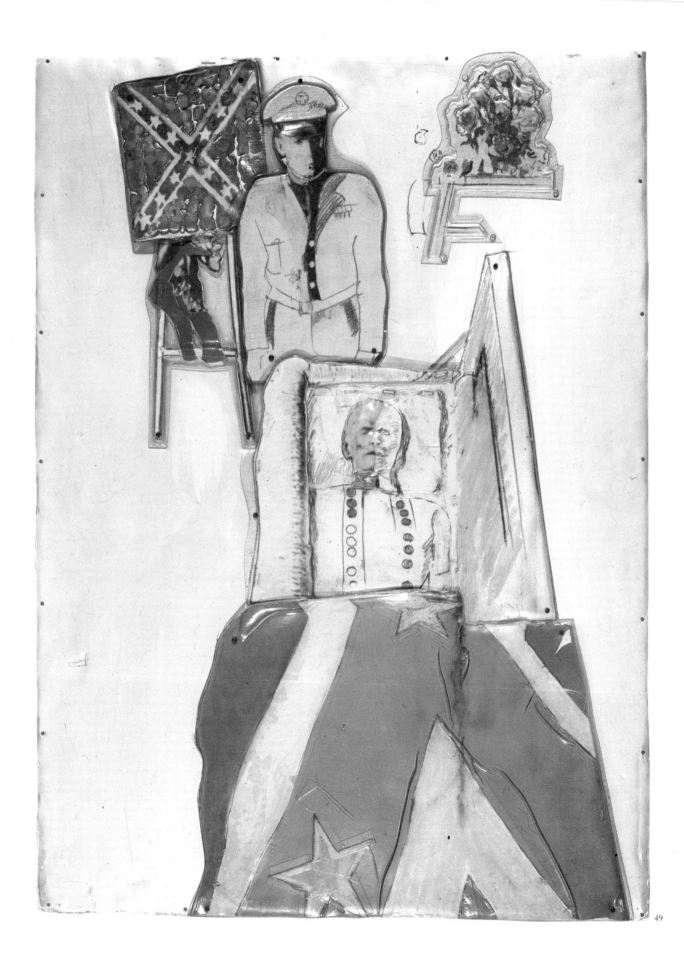

50

49. **Study for Last Civil War Veteran**
    1970
    Mixed media, 31¼ x 23½″
    Private collection

50. **The Ghetto Stoop**
    1969
    Construction, 13′6″ x 10′4″ x 8′10″
    Menil Foundation, Houston, Texas

52

51. **America's Number One Problem**
    1969
    Electrified mixed media construction, 26½ x 20½ x 5″
    Collection the artist

52. **I Like Olympia in Black Face**
    1970
    Mixed media construction, 71⅜ x 76⅜ x 39⅜″
    Collection Musée National d'Art Moderne,
    Centre Georges Pompidou, Paris

page 110
53. **Some American History: African Continent
    and African**
    1970
    Construction, 67 x 64 x 12½″
    Menil Foundation, Houston Texas

page 111
54. **The Divers**
    1968-72
    Mixed media construction 96 x 70 x 7″
    Collection the artist

53

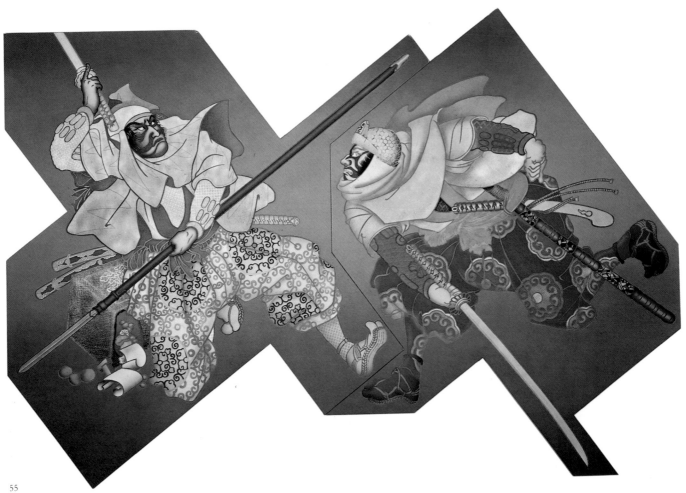

55

55. **Heroes of Chushingura**
1974
Acrylic on canvas, 97 x 138″
Arnold Gallery, Atlanta, Georgia

56. **Kinko the Nymph Bringing Happy Tidings**
1974
Acrylic on canvas, 78 x 108″
The Gund Art Foundation
Cambridge, Massachusetts

58

57. **Utamaro's Women**
    1975
    Acrylic on canvas, 72¾ x 56¾″
    Private collection

58. **Beauty and the Beast II**
    1975
    Pencil on paper, 70¾ x 778¼″
    Collection Harry Horn, Nairobi

page 116
59. **Mixed Patriotic Stamps**
    1976
    Acrylic on canvas, 48 x 36″
    Private collection

page 117
60. **Poem and Portrait: John Ashbery**
    1977
    Acrylic on canvas, 76 x 58″
    Collection the artist

Pyrography

Out here on Cottage Grove it matters. The galloping
Wind balks at its shadow. The carriages
Are drawn forward under a sky of fumed oak.
This is America calling:
The mirroring of state to state,
Of voice to voice on the wires,
The force of colloquial greetings like golden
Pollen sinking on the afternoon breeze.
In service stairs the sweet corruption thrives;
The page of dusk turns like a creaking revolving stage
in Warren, Ohio.

If this is the way it is let's leave,
They agree, and soon the slow boxcar journey begins,
Gradually accelerating until the gyrating fans of suburbs
Enfolding the darkness of cities are remembered
Only as a recurring tic. And midway
We meet the disappointed, returning ones, without its
Being able to stop us in the headlong night
Toward the nothing of the coast. At Bolinas
The houses doze and seem to wonder why through the
Pacific haze, and the dreams alternately glow and grow dull.
Why be hanging on here? Like kites, circling,
Slipping on a ramp of air, but always circling?

But the variable cloudiness is pouring it on,
Flooding back to you like the meaning of a joke.
The land wasn't immediately appealing; we built it
Partly over with fake ruins, in the image of ourselves:
An arch that terminates in mid-keystone, a crumbling stone
For laundresses, an open-air theater, never completed
And only partially designed. How are we to inhabit
This space from which the fourth wall is invariably missing,
As in a stage-set or dollhouse, except by staying as we are,
In lost profile, facing the stars, with a strict sense
Unrealized projects, and a strict sense
Of time running out, of evening presenting
The tactfully folded-over bill? And we fit
Rather too easily into it, become transparent,
Almost ghosts. One day
The birds and animals in the pasture have ab
the density of the surroundings,
alive, and too heavy with lif

(Pyrography--p. 2)

A long period of adjustment followed.
In the cities at the turn of the century they knew about it
But were careful not to let on as the iceman and the milkman
Disappeared down the block and the postman shouted
His daily rounds. The children under the trees knew it
But all the fathers returning home
On streetcars after a satisfying day at the office undid it:
The climate was still floral and all the wallpaper
In a million homes all over the land conspired to hide it.
One day we thought of painted furniture, of how
It just slightly changes everything in the room
And in the yard outside, and how, if we were going
To be able to write the history of our time, starting with today,
It would be necessary to model all these unimportant details
So as to be able to include them; otherwise the narrative
Would have that flat, sandpapered look the sky gets
Out in the middle west toward the end of summer,
The look of wanting to back out before the argument
Has been resolved, and at the same time to save appearances
So that tomorrow will be pure. Therefore, since we have to
In spite of things, why not make it in spite of everything?
That way, maybe the feeble lakes and swamps
Of the back country will get plugged into the circuit
And not just the major events but the whole incredible
Mass of everything happening simultaneously and pairing off,
Channeling itself into history, will unroll
As carefully and as casually as a conversation in the next room,
And the purity of today will invest us like a breeze,
Only be hard, spare, ironical: something one can
Tip one's hat to and still get some use out of.

parade is turning into our street.
stars, the burnished uniforms and prismatic
res of this instant belong here. The land
lling away from the magic, glittering coastal towns
aforementioned rendezvous with August and December.
unch is it will always be this way,
ok, the way things first scared you,
ight light, and later turned out to be,
able, all the same, of a narrow fidelity
unravelling
beyond
se.

61

61. **Rainbow Rembrandt**
1977
Acrylic on canvas, 66 x 76"
Collection The Joseph H. Hirshhorn Museum
and Sculpture Garden, Washington, D.C.

62

62. **Rainbow Rembrandt II**
1977
Acrylic on canvas, 66 x 76"
Private collection

63

63. **Golden Oldies 50s**
1978
Oil and mixed media on canvas and plywood
106 x 144"
Private collection

64. **Golden Oldies: The Greatest Homosexual**
1978
Acrylic and colored pencil on paper, 86 x 56"
Collection Mr. David Sawyers
Stony Creek, Connecticut

64

65

65. **Graph Camel**
1978
Acrylic on canvas, 36 x 36″
Private collection

66

66. **Golden Oldies: French Vocabulary Lesson**
1978
Acrylic, pencil and colored pencil on paper
30¼ x 24¼"
Collection Mr. Simon Daro Dawidowicz
Miami Beach, Florida

67

67. **Portrait of Daniel Webster on a Flesh Field II**
1979
Acrylic on canvas, 74 x 80″
Virginia Museum of Fine Arts
Richmond, Virginia

68

68. **Wedding Photo** (On Approval)
1979
Acrylic on canvas, 38 x 44″
Sidney and Francis Lewis Foundation
Richmond, Virginia

69

70

69. **Beyond Camels**
1980
Acrylic on canvas, 98 x 79″
Private collection

70. **Front and Back Camel**
1980
Pastel and graphite on paper, 16½ x 25″
Private collection

page 128
71. **Golden Oldies: Dutch Masters**
1978
Charcoal and acrylic on paper, 89 x 57″
Collection Sivia and Jeffrey H. Loria, New York

page 129
72. **Syndics of the Drapery Guild as Dutch Masters**
1978-79
Acrylic on canvas and board, 98½ x 69½ x 5½″
Private collection

71

73

page 130

73. **Boucher's Punishment**
1981
Acrylic on canvas, 70 x 48½"
Collection the artist

page 131

74. **The Continuing Interest in Abstract Art: Cutting**
1981
Relief: pencil and colored pencil on paper, 30⅛ x 22¼"
Marlborough Gallery, New York

76

75. **The Continuing Interest in Abstract Art:
   From Photos of Gwynne and Emma Rivers**
   1981
   Mixed media, 78⅛ x 80¾"
   Jan Turner Gallery, Los Angeles, California

76. **The Continuing Interest in Abstract Art: Letters
   from Jean Tinguely and Niki de Saint-Phalle**
   1981
   Acrylic on canvas, 78⅛ x 83⅜"
   Collection the artist

77

77. **The Continuing Interest in Abstract Art:**
Tinguely's Letter
1981
Relief, 29 x 27½"
Private collection

78

78. **The Continuing Interest in Abstract Art:
Now and Then**
1981
Acrylic on canvas
76⅛ x 80½"
Collection Roland and Eleanor Miller, Courtesy
J.B. Speed Museum, Louisville, Kentucky

79

79. **The Continuing Interest in Abstract Art: on the Phone I**
1981
Acrylic on canvas, 52 x 77"
Van Straaten Gallery, Chicago, Illinois

80. **The Continuing Interest in Abstract Art: Sketches with Self-Portrait**
1981
Acrylic on canvas, 56 x 44"
Private collection

81

81. **The Continuing Interest in Abstract Art: Sheila**
1981
Acrylic on canvas, 76⅛ x 80½″
Collection Roland and Eleanor Miller, Courtesy
J.B. Speed Museum, Louisville Kentucky

82

82. **The Continuing Interest in Abstract Art: Posing**
1981
Pencil and colored pencil, 28 x 21⅛″
Private collection

83

83. **The Continuing Interest in Abstract Art:
The Collector**
1981
Relief: Pencil and color pencil on paper
42¼ x 29 x 2″
Collection the artist

84

84. **Dear Dale**
1973-82
Oil on canvas, 70 x 83″
Private collection

85

86

85. **History of Matzoh** (The Story of the Jews)
Part II
1983
Oil on canvas, 120 x 168"
Collection Sivia and Jeffrey H. Loria, New York

86. **History of Matzoh** (The Story of the Jews)
Part II
1983 (study)
Private collection

142

87

88

87. **History of Matzoh** (The Story of the Jews)
Part III
1983
Acrylic on canvas, 116¼ x 180″
Collection Sivia and Jeffrey H. Loria, New York

88. **History of Matzoh** (The Story of the Jews)
Part III
1983 (study)
Private collection

89

89. **Out**
1983
Pencil and colored pencil
33¼ x 29¼″
Private collection

90. **Bad Bird**
1983
Oil on canvas mounted on sculpted foamcore
62 x 49″
Collection the artist

144

91

91. **An Old Sicilian Story**
   1984
   Relief, oil on canvas mounted on sculpted foamcore
   79 x 116″
   Private collection

92

92. **From Picnic Photo**
1985
Oil on canvas mounted on sculpted foamcore
58½ x 73″
Private collection

94

93. **Cubism Today: Striped Face**
    1985
    Oil on canvas mounted on sculpted foamcore
    42 x 30¼"
    Collection Mr. and Mrs. Ben Frankel
    Philadelphia, Pennsylvania

94. **1924 and Matisse**
    1985
    Oil on canvas mounted on sculpted foamcore
    96 x 120"
    Elaine Horwitch Gallery, Santa Fe, New Mexico

96

95. **Desert Scene Relief**
1985
Mixed media, oil on canvas, relief on foamcore
51 x 41″
Heland Thorden Wetterling Galleries, New York

96. **Entwined Figures**
1985
Relief, oil on canvas, 50 x 65″
Collection Sivia and Jeffrey H. Loria, New York

page 152
97. **Dutch Masters Box**
1985
Mixed media relief, paper and colored pencil on
paper, mounted on sculpted foamcore, 82¾ x 57 x 21¼″
Private collection

page 153
98. **The Peaceful Past**
1985
Colored pencil, 33 x 31″
Private collection

151

98

99

99. **25 Birds of the Northeast**
    1985-86
    Oil on canvas mounted on sculpted foamcore
    58 x 80½″
    Simms Fine Art, New York

100. **Planned Parenthood**
    1986
    Oil on canvas mounted on sculpted foamcore
    100 x 80″
    Collection the artist

155

101

101. **Kinko the Nymph**
1985-86
Acrylic on canvas mounted on foamcore
32 x 64 x 4″
Collection The Gund Art Foundation
Cambridge, Massachusetts

102. **Matisse Opera and the Continuous Line**
1986
Oil on canvas mounted on sculpted foamcore
68 x 56″
Collection Frederick Weisman Co.,
Baltimore, Maryland

156

103

103. Chinese Information: Female Rider
1983-1986
Oil on canvas mounted on sculpted foamcore
36 x 36"
Private collection

104

104. **Chinese Information: Male Rider**
1983-1986
Oil on canvas mounted on sculpted foamcore
36 x 36″
Jan Turner Gallery, Los Angeles, California

105. **Duck Farm Relief: Umber Pants**
1986
Oil on canvas mounted on sculpted foamcore
47 x 42″
Collection Mr. and Mrs. Myron Beigler
Los Altos, California

106

106. **A Vanished World: Trnava, Czecholsovakia, 1936**
Raising Geese I
1987
Oil on canvas, mounted on foamcore, 65½ x 60 x 5″
Private collection

108

107. **Relief from Berdie Photo**
     1986
     Mixed media relief, 53 x 43″
     Private collection

108. **Work and Portrait of Red Grooms**
     1986
     Oil on canvas mounted on sculpted foamcore
     64 x 61″
     Collection Mr. and Mrs. Robert Schniler
     Boca Raton, Florida

109

109. **Back to Back I**
1986
Oil on canvas mounted on sculpted foamcore
34 x 48"
Collection Marcia Levine, New York

110. **Dancing with the Dancer, II**
1986
Oil on canvas, 28½ x 23"
Collection Mr. and Mrs. Sidney R. Onobskey
San Francisco, California

111. **Make Believe Ballroom, Rita's Red Dress**
1987
Oil on canvas mounted on sculpted foamcore
57¼ x 51 x 4″
Private collection

112

112. **Make Believe Ballroom: The Dip**
1987
Oil on canvas mounted on sculpted foamcore
60¾ x 65½"
Private collection

113.

113. **A Song to the Avant-Garde I**
1987
Pencil and collage on paper, 10½ x 11″
Collection the artist

114. **A Song to the Avant-Garde II**
1987
Pencil and collage on paper, 10¼ x 10½″
Collection the artist

115. **A Song to the Avant-Garde III**
1987
Pencil and collage on paper, 10⅛ x 10½″
Collection the artist

116. **A song to the Avant-Garde IV**
1987
Pencil and collage on paper, 15¾ x 16⅛″
Collection the artist

117. **A Song to the Avant-Garde V**
1987
Pencil and collage on paper, 16 x 15⅝″
Collection the artist

118. **A song to the Avant-Garde VI**
1987
Pencil and collage on paper, 15¾ x 15⅞″
Collection the artist

119. **A Song to the Avant-Garde VII**
1987
Pencil and collage on paper, 15¾ x 15⅞″
Collection the artist

114-115

116-117

118-119

120. **A Song to the Avant-Garde VIII**
1987
Pencil and collage on paper, 15⅝ x 15¾"
Collection the artist

121

121. **Portrait of Paula Gordon**
1987
Oil on canvas mounted on sculpted foamcore
64 x 70¼″
Collection Mr. and Mrs. Edward Gordon, New York

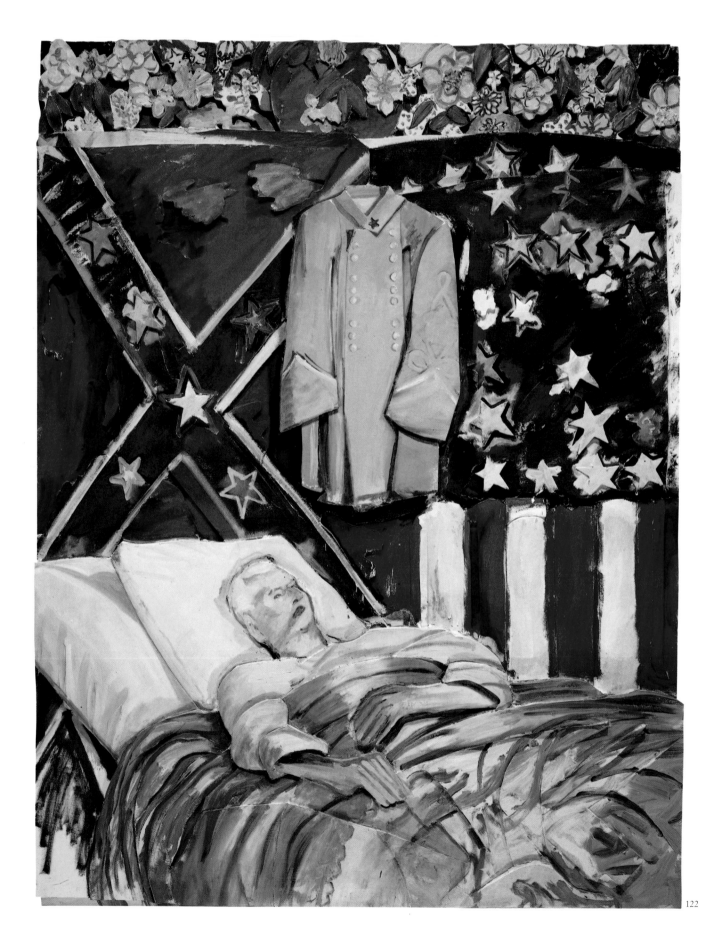

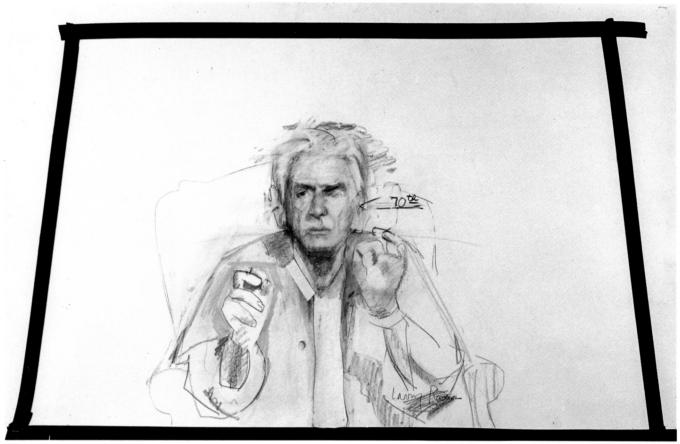

123

122. **Last Civil War Veteran: Indigo Blue**
1987
Oil on canvas mounted on sculpted foamcore
75¼ x 57½ x 5"
Collection the artist

123. **Portrait of Leonard Bernstein**
1987
Pastel and color pencil, 11 x 18"
Private collection

124

124. **Umber Blues II, Sonny on the Side Relief**
1987
Oil on canvas mounted on sculpted foamcore
34 x 49″
Collection the artist

125

125. **Dick Schwartz, Umber Blues**
1987
Oil on canvas, 64½ x 79″
Private collection

126

126. **Daniel Webster Amidst the Cigar Box Paraphernalia**
1987
Acrylic on canvas, 74 x 80⅛"
Private collection

127

127. **Dancer in an Abstract Field: Merce Spreading I**
1988
Oil on canvas mounted on sculpted foamcore
33½ x 56½ x 2½″
Private collection

128

128. **Dancer in an Abstract Field: Merce Spreading II**
1988
Oil on canvas mounted on sculpted foamcore
33½ x 56½ x 2½″
Private collection

129

129. **Dancer in an Abstract Field: Susan Bending**
1988
Oil on canvas mounted on sculpted foamcore
39 x 45½ x 2½″
Private collection

130

130. **Dancer in an Abstract Field: Fred Twisting I**
1988
Oil on canvas mounted on sculpted foamcore
39½ x 43½"
Private collection

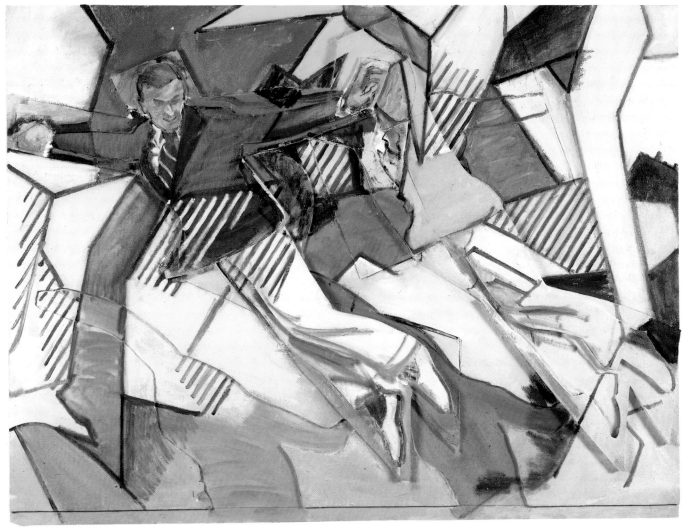

131

131. **Dancer in an Abstract Field: Fred Flying I**
1988
Oil on canvas mounted on sculpted foamcore
40¾ x 54¾ x 2½"
Private collection

132

132. **Seventy-Five Years
Later: Naples**
1988
Oil on canvas
mounted on
sculpted foamcore
74¼ x 47½ x 3″
Private collection

182

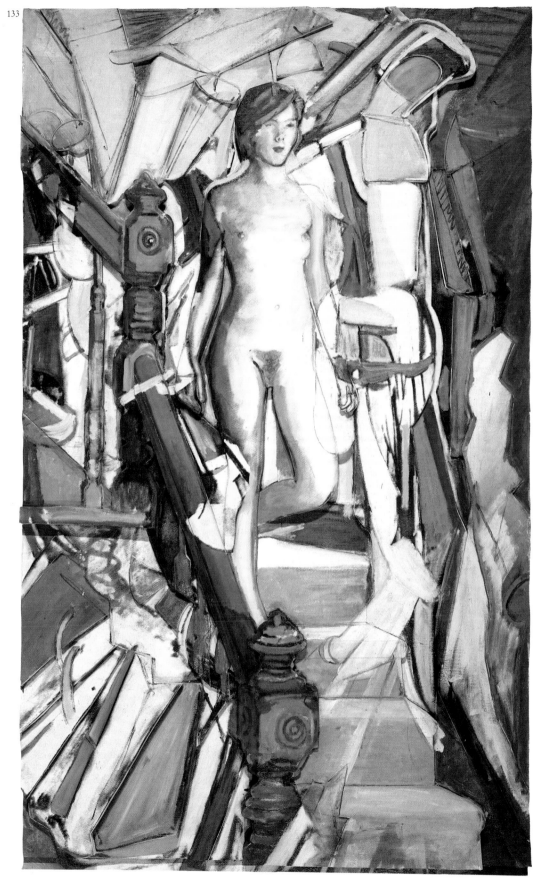

133. **Seventy-Five Years Later: Indigo**
1988
Oil on canvas
mounted on
sculpted foamcore
71 x 44 x 4″
Collection
Peter Lewis
Cleveland, Ohio

135

134. **Primo Levi I**
1988
Oil on canvas mounted on sculpted foamcore
73 x 58½ x 4"
Collection La Stampa, Turin, Italy

135. **Primo Levi: Witness**
1988
Oil on canvas mounted on sculpted foamcore
58½ x 33 x 4"
Collection La Stampa, Turin, Italy

BLACK & WHITE PLATES

136

137

138

136. **Football Players**
     1951
     Oil and collage, 42 x 47½″
     Collection Mr. and Mrs Oscar L. Gerber
     Highland Park, Illinois

137. **Reclining Female Figure**
     Bronze, 6½ x 16″
     Collection the artist

138. **Berdie**
     1952
     Bronze, 31½″ high
     Collection the artist

139. **Self-portrait**
     1953
     Pastel and black chalk, 28½ x 21″
     Art Institute of Chicago, Illinois

139

140

140. **Self Figure**
1953
Oil on canvas, 93⅜ x 65½"
The Corcoran Gallery of Art, Washington, D.C.

141. **Female Nude and Floor**
1953
(restored, 1956)
Plaster and wood planks, 68" high
Collection the artist

142. **Head of a Man**
1953
Bronze, 16½ x 7 x 11"
Collection the artist

143

144

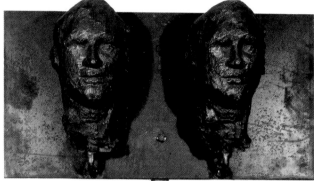

143. **Berdie in the Garden**
    1954
    Oil on canvas, 61¾ x 50¼″
    Collection David Daniels, New York

144. **Woman with Cat**
    1954
    Oil on canvas
    Private collection

145. **Double Portrait of John Myers**
    1954
    Bronze, 72″ high with base
    Collection David P. Bassine, New York

145

146

147

148

146. **Child with Dolls**
Oil on canvas
1956
24 x 18″
Collection the artist

147. **Southampton Backyard**
1956
Oil on canvas, 35⅜ x 40″
Private collection

148. **The Athlete's Dream**
1956
Oil on canvas, 82 x 128″
National Museum of American Art
Smithsonian Institution, Washington, D.C.

149. **Bedroom**
1955
Oil on canvas, 85 x 71½″
Collection Dr. Frank M. Purnell, New York

149

150

151

152

150. **Portrait of Dr. Kenneth Wright**
1956
17½ x 20¾″
Collection Dorothy Wright
Southampton, New York

151. **Comic Collaboration with Kenneth Koch**
1956
Gouache and mixed media, 19 x 24″
Private collection

152. **Portrait of Betty Weisberger**
1957
Oil on canvas, 27½ x 35″
Collection Mr. and Mrs. Donald M. Weisberger
New York

153. **Jazz Musician**
1958
Oil on canvas, 70 x 58″
Private collection

153

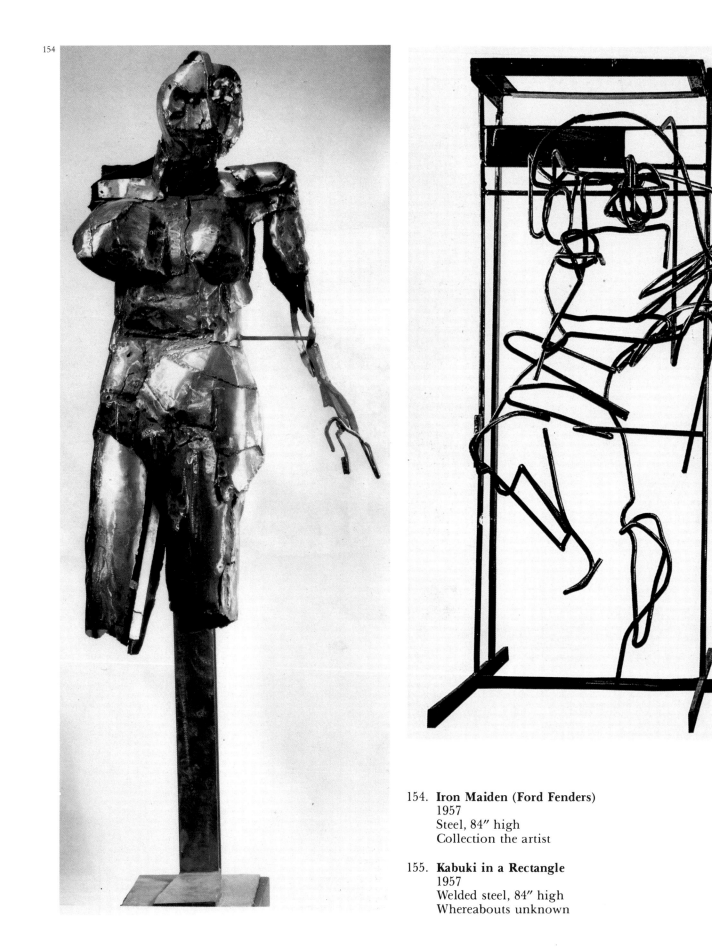

154

155

154. **Iron Maiden (Ford Fenders)**
1957
Steel, 84" high
Collection the artist

155. **Kabuki in a Rectangle**
1957
Welded steel, 84" high
Whereabouts unknown

156

156. The Wall
1957
Oil on canvas, 32 x 44″
Collection Mrs. Lloyd H. Smith, New York

157

158

159

160

157. **Red Molly**
1957
Oil on canvas, 69 x 58″
Collection Mr. and Mrs. Selig S. Burrows
New York

158. **Untitled**
1958
Oil on canvas, 46 x 44¾″
Collection the artist

159. **Night Painting and Maxine**
1958
Oil and charcoal on linen, 72⅛ x 60¼″
The Hirshhorn Museum and Sculpture Garden
Washington, D.C.

160. **Summer 1958, Maxine**
1958
Oil on canvas, 24½ x 32″
Collection Mr. and Mrs. Guy Weill
Scarsdale, New York

161

161. **The Welding Wall**
1958
Oil on canvas, 71½ x 81½″
Collection Mr. and Mrs. Donald M. Weisberger
New York

162

162. **Pots and Pans**
1958
Oil on canvas, 47 x 41″
Collection Mr. and Mrs. I. Nelson, New York

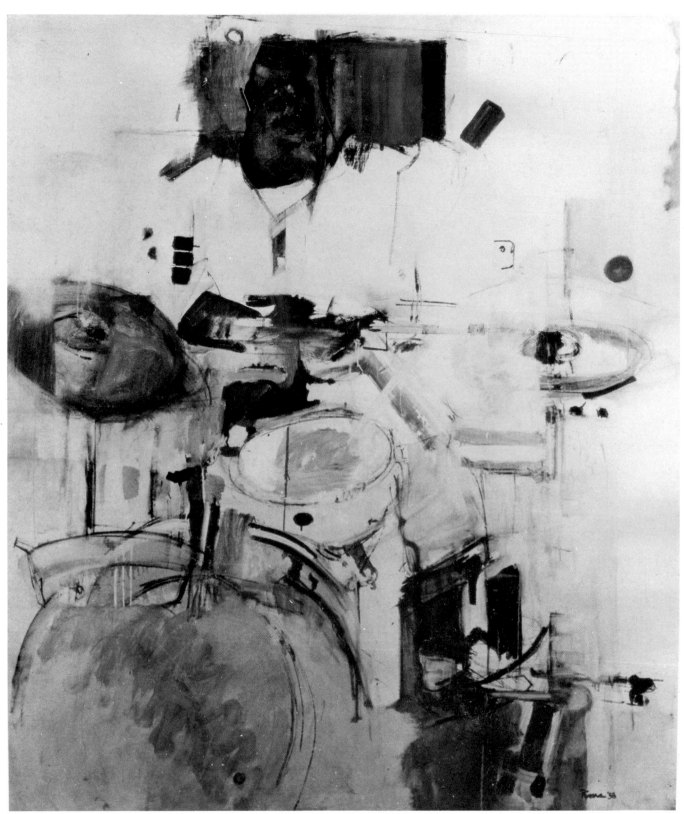

163

163. **The Drummer.**
1958
Oil on canvas, 68 x 58″
Collection Mr. and Mrs. Guy Weill, Scarsdale, New York

164

164. **Second Avenue with "The"**
1958
Oil on canvas, 72¾ x 82¾"
Collection Mr. and Mrs. Patrick B. McGinnis
Cincinnati, Ohio

165. **Miss New Jersey**
1959
Oil on canvas, 60 x 48"
Private collection

166. **Horses**
1959
Oil on canvas, 79 x 60"
Collection Stanley Bard, New York

165

166

167

168

167. **Jack of Spades**
1960
Oil on canvas, 24 x 18″
Collection the artist

168. **Cousin**
1960
Oil on canvas, 60 x 52″
Private collection

169

170

169. **Dougherty Ace of Spades**
1960
Oil on canvas, 74 x 56″
Museum of Art, Fort Lauderdale, Florida

170. **Washington Crossing the Delaware II**
1960
Oil on canvas, 7 x 9′
Whitney Museum of American Art, New York

171

172

171. **New York, 1950-60**
(collaboration with Kenneth Koch)
1961
Oil on canvas, 69 x 84″
Private collection

172. **Disque Bleu**
1961
Oil on canvas, 13 x 13″
Collection the artist

173. **Turning Friendship of America and France**
1961
Oil on canvas with motorized stand, 26¾ x 17 x 11½″
Collection the artist

174. **Portrait of Howard Kanovitz**
1960
Oil on canvas on wood, 19¼ x 21¼″
Collection Arthur Paul, Chicago, Illinois

173

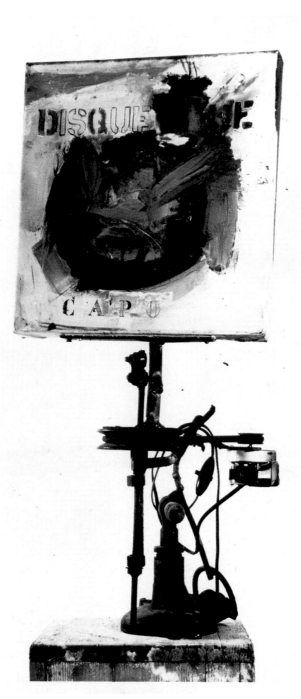

174

page 212
175. **Cedar Bar Menu II**
1961
Oil on canvas, 48¼ x 36″
Collection Mr. and Mrs. Richard Titelman
Atlanta, Georgia

page 213
176. **Marriage Photograph II**
1961
Oil on canvas, 77 x 60″
Collection the artist

MENU

BEAN SOUP – .35
w/ORDER – .25

BEEF _____ w/NOODLES – 1.25
LAMB SHANK – 1.00

HAWAIIAN HAM STEAK – 1.35
_____ – 1.05
_____ – .90

LIMA B__'s   BOIL. POTS.
SALAD   HOME FRYS

antine

176

177

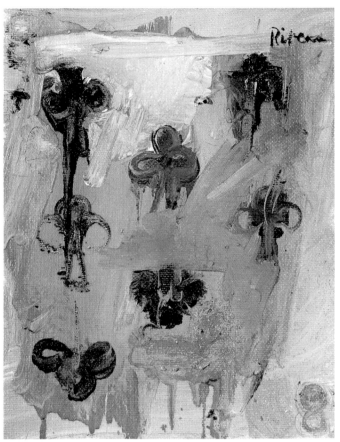

178

177. **Mr. Art (Portrait of David Sylvester)**
1962
Oil on canvas, 72 x 52″
Private collection

178. **Eight of Clubs**
1961
Oil and charcoal on canvas, 10⅛ x 8⅛″
Collection the artist

179. **Parts of the Face: French**
1961
Oil board on relief, 11¼ x 11¼″
Private collection

179

page 216
180. **Study for Civil War Veteran, Dead**
1961
Collage and pencil, paint and assorted papers
17 x 14″
Collection Mr. and Mrs. Marco di Laurenti
New York

page 217
181. **Parts of the Body: French Vocabulary Lesson**
1961-62
Oil on canvas, 72 x 48″
Private collection

180

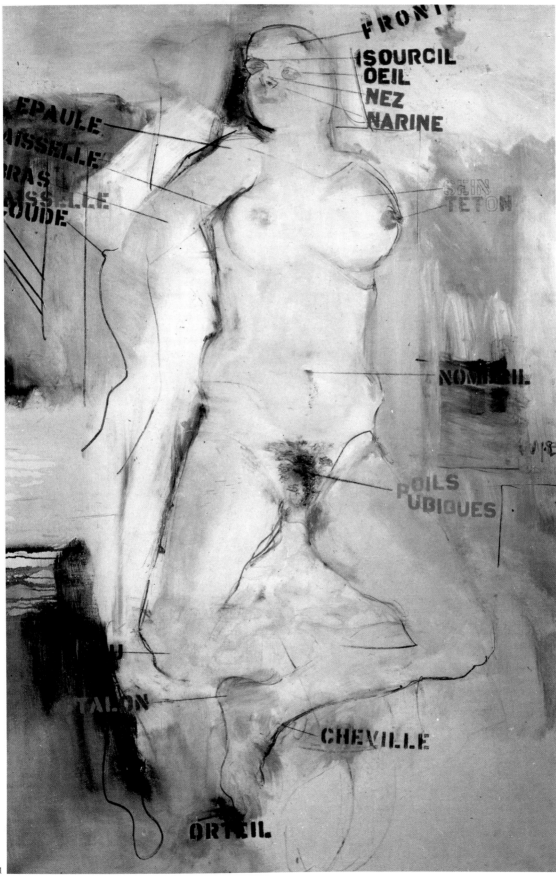

181

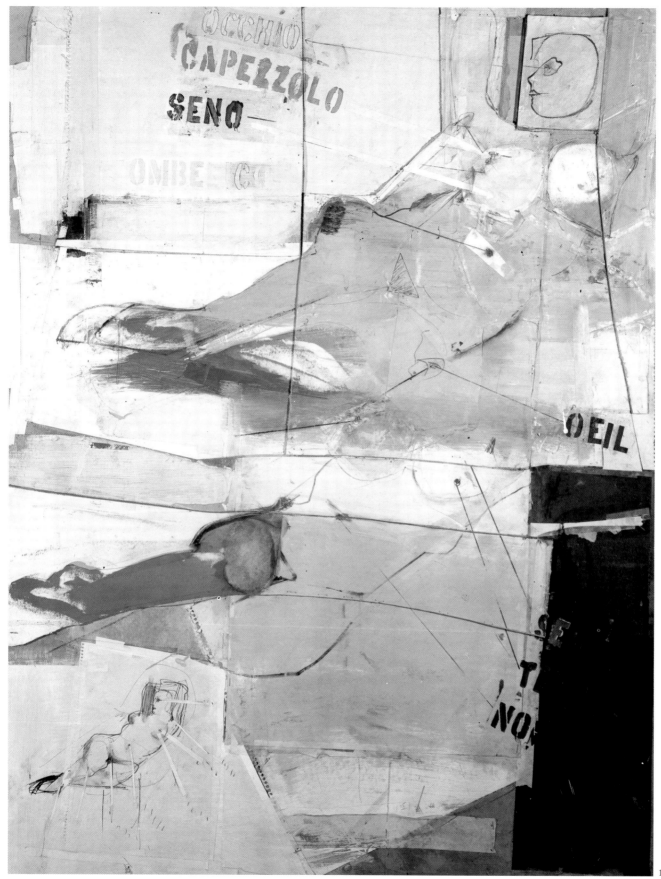

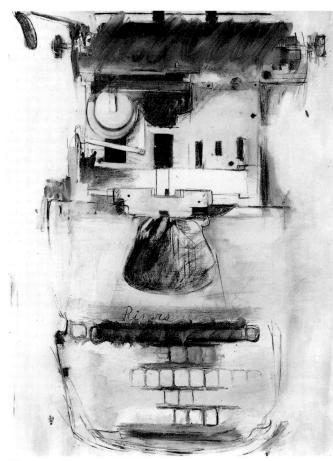

183

184

182. **Parts of the Body**
    (French and Italian Vocabulary)
    1963
    Oil and collage on board, 51½ x 40″
    Collection the artist

183. **Typewriter Painting**
    1962
    Oil on canvas, 57½ x 45″
    Private collection

184. **Yeux: Parts of the Face**
    1962
    Oil and collage on canvas
    Private collection

185

186

185. **First New York Film Festival Billboard**
1963
Oil on canvas, 9′6″ x 15′
The Hirshhorn Museum and Sculpture Garden
Washington, D.C.

186. **Portrait of Dr. Bernard Brodsky**
1963
Oil on canvas, 65 x 48″
Collection Dr. and Mrs. Bernard Brodsky, New York

187

187. **Dutch Masters, Presidents**
1963
Oil on board and collage, 30 x 35½″
Private collection

188

189

188. **Barbara Goldsmith: Echoes and Parts**
1963
Oil and collage on canvas, 68 x 80"
Collection C. Gerald Goldsmith, New York

189. **Moon Man and Moon Lady**
1963
Oil on canvas, 46 x 68"
Private collection

190. **Here Lies Shakespeare**
1963
Oil and collage on board, 60 x 40"
Private collection

191

224

192

191. **Window Webster**
1963
Collage on board, 60 x 40″
Collection the artist

192. **The Greeks**
1963
Bronze, h. 132″
Collection the artist

193. **Notes**
1964
Mixed media, 38¾ x 30¼″
Private collection

193

194

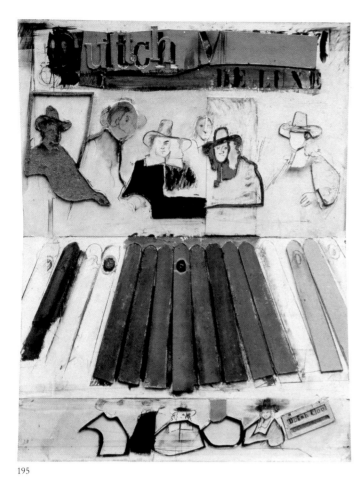

195

196

194. **Dutch Masters Presidents Relief**
1964
Oil and collage on canvas mounted on wood box
98 x 69½ x 12″
Private collection

195. **Dutch Masters Relief**
1964
Oil and collage on board, mounted on wood
32⅝ x 26 x 7¾″
Private collection

196. **Dutch Masters (Corona)**
1964
Oil and collage on canvas, 35½ x 25″
Collection Jacques Kaplan, New York

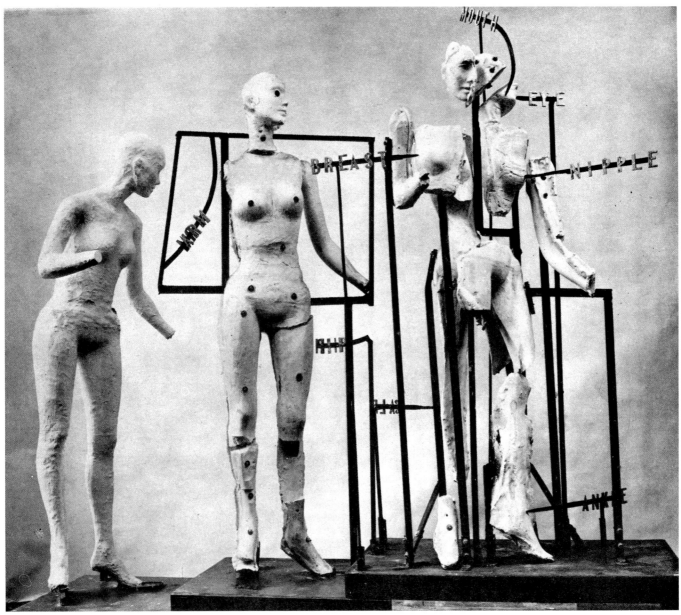

197

197. **Parts of the Body: English Vocabulary Lesson**
1964
Plaster and steel, 83¾ x 90½ x 24¼″
Collection the artist

198

198. **Electric Webster**
1964
Oil, plexiglas, collage and electric light, 30 x 44″
Collection Jacques Kaplan, New York

199. **The Identification Manual** (closed)
1964
Oil and collage on canvas, 47 x 30″
Collection Container Corporation
of America

200. **The Identification Manual** (open)
1964
Oil and assemblage on canvas
left panel: 32 x 25″
center panel: 72 x 52″
Collection Container Corporation
of America

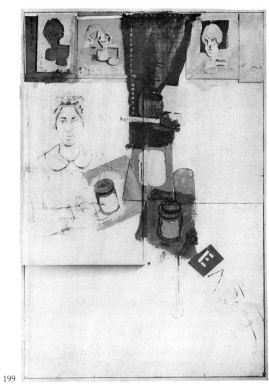

199

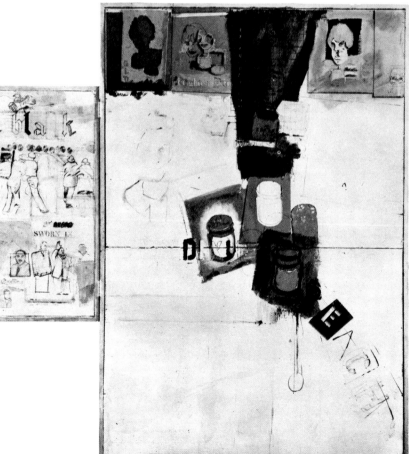

200

201

203

202

201. **The Second Greatest Homosexual** (discards)
1965
Oil and collage on paper, 24 x 15¾"
Collection Mr. and Mrs. Scott Hodes
Chicago, Illinois

202. **Six Flowers**
1965
Oil on board relief, 14½ x 16"
Private collection

203. **Lions on the Dreyfus Fund IV**
1964
Oil and collage, stencil cut-out on canvas, 60½ x 60½"
Private collection

page 232
204. **The History of the Russian Revolution from Marx to Mayakovsky** (detail)
1965
Mixed media construction, 53 pieces, 14'4" x 32'5" x 18"
The Hirshhorn Museum and Sculpture Garden
Washington, D.C.

204

205. **The Second Greatest Homosexual**
1965
Mixed media, 74½ x 62½″
Collection the artist

206. **Tinguely (Storm Window)**
1965
Oil and collage on board with storm window
29 x 25 x 23¾″
Collection the artist

207. **Portrait of Herbert Lee**
1965
Relief, mixed media, 74½ x 54 x 13″
Collection Mr. and Mrs. Herbert C. Lee
Belmont, Massachusetts

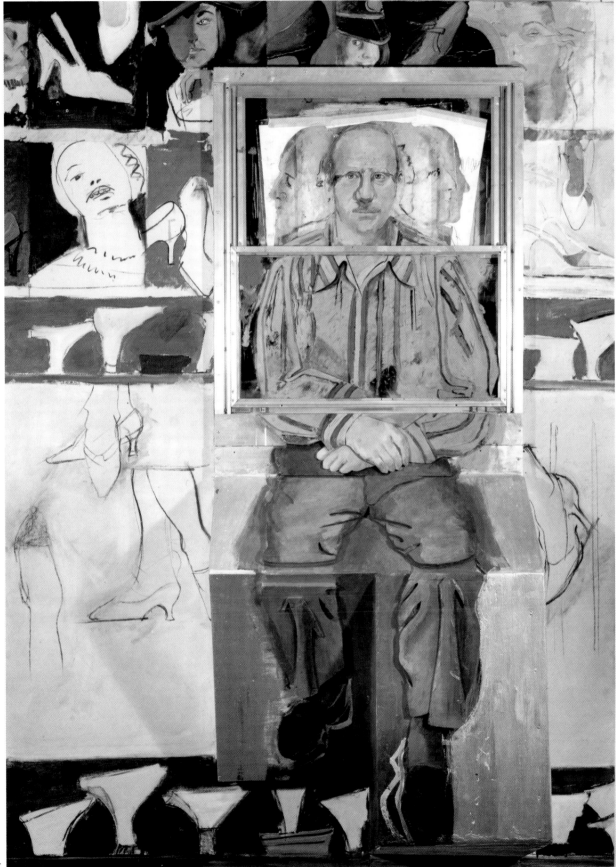

208

209

210.

208. **French Bank Note**
1961-65
Oil on canvas, 34 x 54½ x 5″
Private collection

209. **Don't Fall and Me**
1966
Oil and collage on canvas mounted on wood
16¼ x 28″
Collection the artist

210. **Advertisement for Helene Spitzer**
1966
Oil and collage on canvas, 58 x 59½ x 3″
Collection Mrs. Helene Spitzer, New York

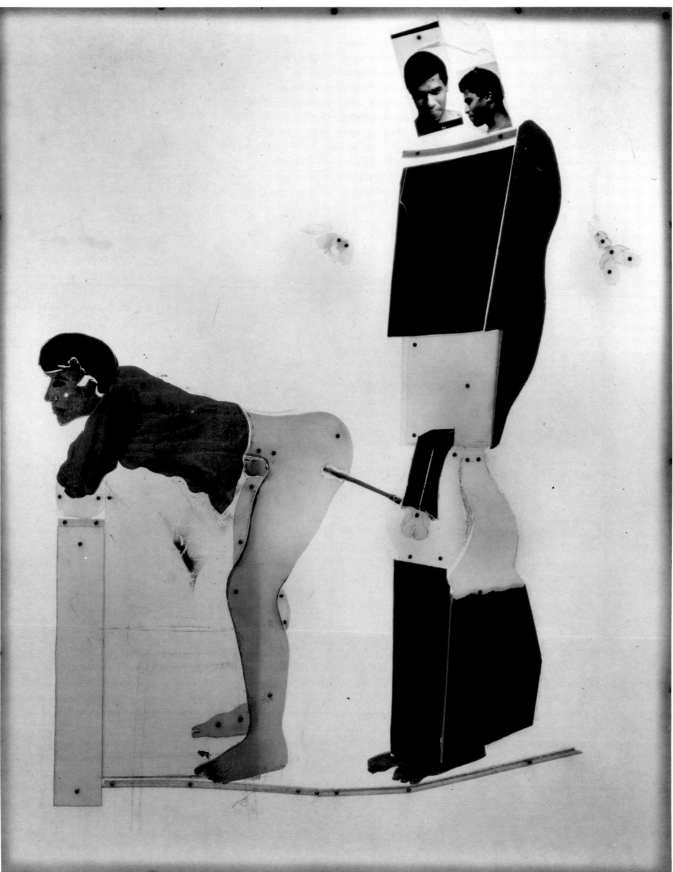

211

212

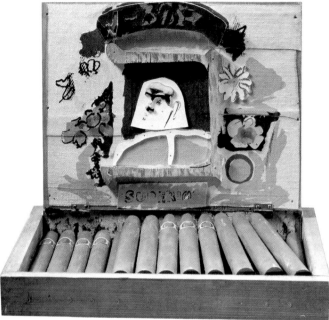

213

211. **Study for "Lamp Man Loves It"**
1966
Plastic and painted wood mounted on wood box
with electric light, 29¾ x 24 x 3⅜"
Collection the artist

212. **Don't Fall**
1966
Electric construction, 34¼ x 24 x 8½"
Collection the artist

213. **Webster and Cigars**
1966
Mixed media, collage on wood construction
13¼ x 16 x 13¼"
Collection the artist

page 240
214. **In Memory of the Dead**
1967
Spray paint and collage in relief, 30 x 21"
Collection the artist

page 241
215. **Covering the Earth**
1967
Mixed media, 48 x 37½ x 18"
Marlborough Gallery, New York

215

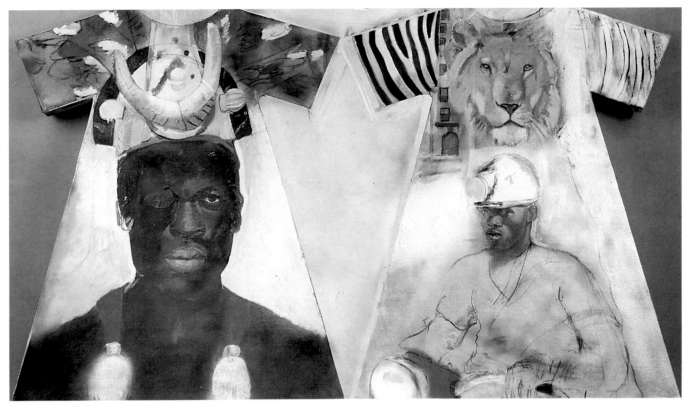

216

216. **Throwaway Dress: New York to Nairobi**
1967
Oil on canvas and wood construction, 45¾ x 78 x 3″
Marlborough Gallery, New York

217. **Cropped Blue Bed**
1967
Mixed media, 47½ x 48 x 40¾″
Collection the artist

217

242

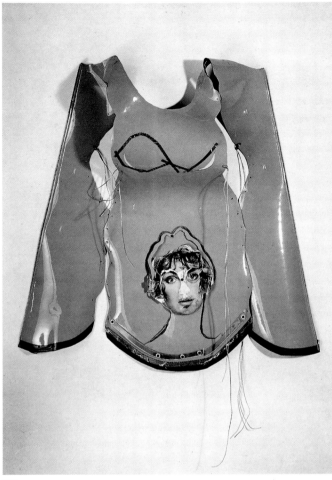

218

219

218. **Shrimpton's Vinyl**
1969
Vinyl and collage, 33″ high
Private collection

219. **Norman Mailer: Study for Time Magazine Cover**
1968
Collage relief, 11½ x 8½″
Collection the artist

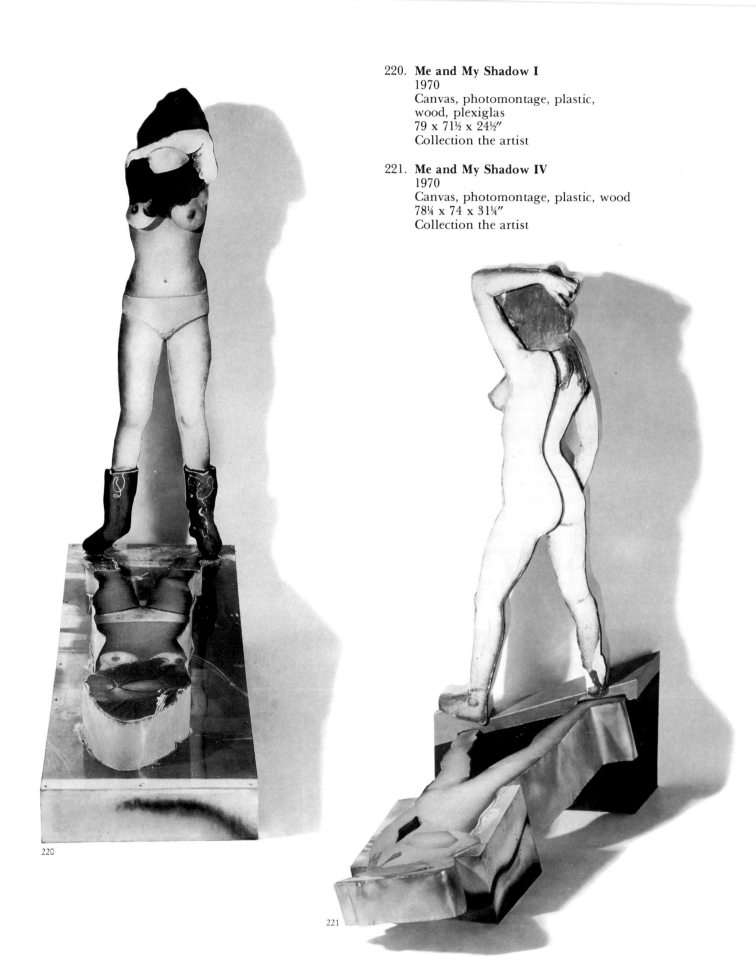

220. **Me and My Shadow I**
1970
Canvas, photomontage, plastic,
wood, plexiglas
79 x 71½ x 24½″
Collection the artist

221. **Me and My Shadow IV**
1970
Canvas, photomontage, plastic, wood
78¼ x 74 x 31¼″
Collection the artist

220

221

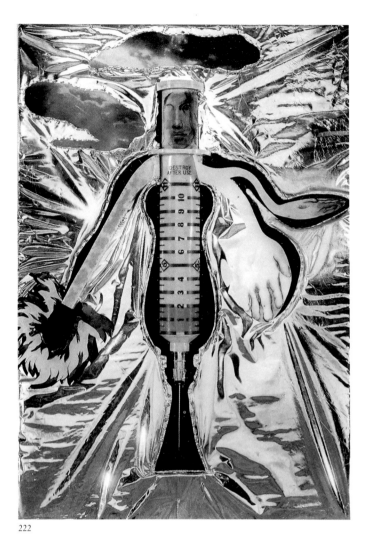

222

224

223

222. **Bad Witch**
1970
Mixed media, 90 x 64″
Collection the artist

223. **Wooden Dutch Masters**
1971
Wood encased in plastic, 10¾ x 16¼″
Private collection

224. **Miss Popcorn**
1972
Acrylic on vinyl, 72 x 43″
Museo de Arte Contemporáneo, Caracas, Venezuela

225. **Umber and Pink Jemima,
Portrait of Hattie McDaniel**
1973
Acrylic on vinyl, 32½ x 48½″
Private collection

226. **Movie House**
1973
Mixed media, air brush, 72¼ x 184¾ x 6″
Private collection

225

226

246

227

227. **Garbage**
1973
Mixed media collage on canvas, 90 x 90"
Butler Institute of American Art,
Youngstown, Ohio
Gift of Professor and Mrs. Sam Hunter

228

228. **Portrait of Miss Oregon II**
1973
Acrylic on canvas, 66 x 108″
Private collection

229. **Beauty and Beast I**
1975
Acrylic on canvas, 114 x 60″
Collection Sivia and Jeffrey H. Loria, New York

229

230

230. **The Stripe is in the Eye of the Beholder**
1975
Acrylic on canvas, 85¾ x 100½"
Private collection

231

231. **The Continuing Interest in Abstract Art:**
Happy Frank, No. 2
1981
Pencil on paper mounted on canvas, 28¾ x 42″
Collection the artist

232

232. **Chinese Information (Travel I)**
1980
Oil on canvas, 120 x 144″
Private collection

233

233. **Chinese Information (Travel II)**
1980
Oil on canvas, 120 x 144"
Private collection

DRAWINGS

234

235

page 256
234. **Portrait of Jane Freilicher**
1950
Pencil on paper, 13½ x 10⅞″
Collection the artist

page 257
235. **Rabbi Reading, Study for "The Burial"**
1951
Charcoal, 16½ x 14″
Collection the artist

236

237

236. **From Rembrandt**
1952
Pencil, 16½ x 13¾″
Collection the artist

237. **Study for "The Burial"**
1951
Charcoal, 14 x 16½″
Collection the artist

238

239

238. **Bathers (after Cézanne)**
1952
Pastel and pencil, 13¾ x 16½"
Collection Mr. and Mrs. George L. Sturman
Chicago, Illinois

239. **After David**
1952
Pencil on paper, 14 x 14"
Collection the artist

240

240. **Study for "Washington Crossing the Delaware"**
1953
Pencil, 11 x 13⅜"
Museum of Modern Art, New York

241

241. **Study for "Washington Crossing the Delaware"**
(two heads and a horse)
1953
Pencil, 11 x 13⅝″
Museum of Modern Art, New York

Rivers 53
Dedicated To
St. Thomas University

History is made by
nervous men

Rivers!!!

242

242. **George Washington**
1953
Pencil and collage, 13⅞ x 15⅜″
Menil Foundation Collection, Houston, Texas

243. **Portrait of John Ashbery**
1953
Pastel, 13¾ x 16¼″
Museum of Modern Art, New York

244. **Portrait of Kenneth Koch**
1953
Pencil, 13¾ x 16¾″
Museum of Modern Art, New York

page 264
245. **Frank O'Hara**
1953
Pencil on paper, 6⅛ x 5⅛″
Museum of Modern Art, New York

page 265
246. **Portrait of Augusta**
1953
Pencil on paper, 14 x 11″
Collection of the artist

243

244

245

247

248

247. **Augusta**
1953
Pencil on paper, 14 x 11″
Collection the artist

248. **Robertus**
1954
Pencil heightened with white gouache, 12 x 14¼″
Collection the artist

249

249. **Edwin Denby**
1953
Pencil on paper, 16⅜ x 19¾"
Museum of Modern Art, New York

250

250. **Joseph Seated**
1954
Pencil on paper, 11 x 14″
Collection Ellen Adler, New York

251. **Frank O'Hara with Boots on Study for "O'Hara"**
1954
Pencil on paper, 24¾ x 18¾″
Collection the artist

Sketch for the O'hara painting
Rivers 1954

252

252. **Berdie Seated on Bed**
1954
Pencil on paper, 18¾ x 24⅞"
Collection the artist

253. **Sonia, the Artist's Mother**
1954
Pencil on paper, 16⅝ x 13¾"
Collection the artist

253

Larry Rivers

Grace Hartigan

254. **Portrait of Grace Hartigan**
1954
Pencil on paper, 25 x 18
Collection Jane Freilicher, New York

255. **Flower Studies after Leonardo** (detail)
1954
Pencil, 13¾ x 10½″ (full size)
Collection the artist

256. **Middle Europe, Double Portrait of Myself**
1954
Pencil on paper, 18½ x 24¼″
Private collection

255

256

257

257. Joan Mitchel in a Summer Hat
1955
Pencil on paper, 13⅞ x 16½"
Collection Richard and Carol Selle
Chicago, Illinois

258. **Head of Joseph**
1956
Pencil, 12 x 9″
Collection the artist

259. **Brushes and Cooper's Hawk**
1956
Pencil on paper, 14 x 16½″
Private collection

260. **Moustache Portrait of Pierre Restenay**
1956
Pencil on paper, 14 x 15″
Collection the artist

258

259

260

261

261. **Child with Dolls**
    1956
    Pencil, 16½ x 13″
    Collection the artist

262. **Frank O'Hara Seated with Hands Clasped**
    1956
    Pencil on paper, 18 x 14½″
    Collection the artist

263. **John Myers**
    1957
    Pencil on paper, 14 x 16⅞″
    Collection the artist

262

263

264

264. **Female Karl Marx**
1959
Pencil on paper, 13⅞ x 16½"
Collection the artist

265. **Stones: US,** collaboration with Frank O'Hara
1958
Lithograph, 24 x 30"
Collection the artist

266. **Rejected Copy**
1978
Pencil and colored paper on paper, 24 x 20"
Private collection

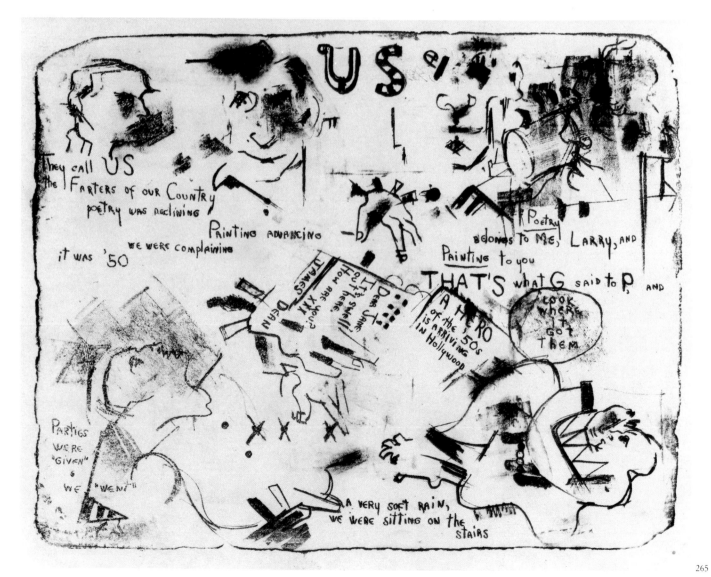

265

266

279

267

267. **The Continuing Interest in Abstract Art:**
Emma and Dad
1981
Pencil and colored pencil on paper, 27½ x 32"
Collection the artist

268

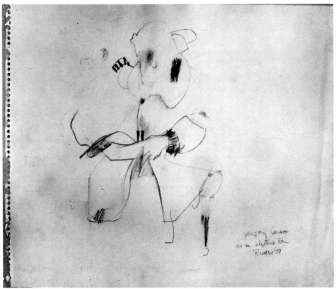

269

270

268. **Stephen (14th Birthday)**
1959
Pencil on paper, 13 x 15″
Collection the artist

269. **Gregory Corso as an Electric Fan**
1959
Pencil, 14 x 17″
Collection the artist

270. **Record Cover for Jack Teagarden**
1960
Pencil and collage on paper, 13⅞ x 13¾″
Columbia Records, New York

page 282
271. **Drawing for Kerouac-Beat**
1960
Pencil, 16½ x 13⅜″
Collection Rotrot Klein Moquit, Phoenix, Arizona

page 283
272. **The Last Civil War Veteran**
1961
Pencil on paper with collage heightened with
white gouache, 10 x 8″
Thomas E. Benesch Memorial Collection
Museum of Art, Baltimore, Maryland

BEAT

Rivers

271

273. **Clarice: Crossed Ankles**
     1961
     Pencil on paper, 11½ x 9″
     Private collection

274. **Small Friendship of America and France**
     1961
     Pencil on paper, 9 x 10½″
     Private collection

273

274

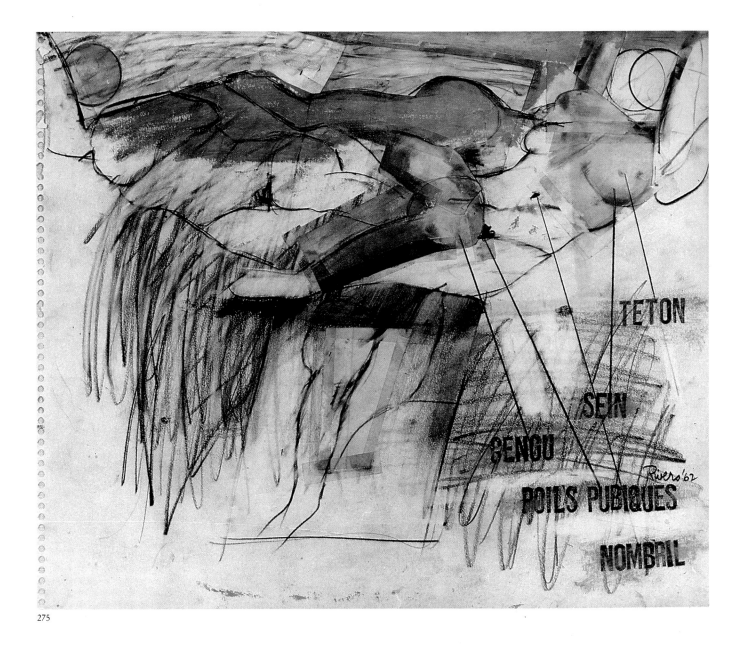

275

TETON

SEIN

GENOU

POILS PUBIQUES

NOMBRIL

Rivers '62

275. **How to Draw Reclining Nudes and**
Rectangles with Legs
1962
Collage and watercolor, 14 x 17″
Private collection

page 286
276. **How to Draw Noses**
1962
Watercolor, pencil and collage, 14⅝ x 12½″
Formerly collection James Thrall Soby
New Canaan, Connecticut

NEZ

NASO

NASE

NOS

276

277

277. Camels
1961
Pencil on paper, 17 x 14"
Private collection

278

279

278. **Study for Second Version of George Washington
Crossing the Delaware,**
1960
Pencil, 19⅞ x 26⅛″
Museum of Modern Art, New York

279. **Transit**
1961
Pencil and collage, 13⅜ x 16⅜″
Private collection

280

280. **How to Draw Series: Oreilles [Ears]**
1962
Collage with gouache, pencil, charcoal,
photomechanical reproduction, and cellophane
tape on paper, 9¼ x 10⅜″
The Hirshhorn Museum and Sculpture Garden
Washington, D.C.

281. **How to Draw Series: Pieds [Feet]**
1962
Collage with gouache, pencil, charcoal,
photomechanical reproduction, and cellophane
tape on paper, 14⅜ x 10½″
The Hirshhorn Museum and Sculpture Garden
Washington, D.C.

282. **Camels**
1962
Pencil on paper, 14½ x 13″
Private collection

281

282

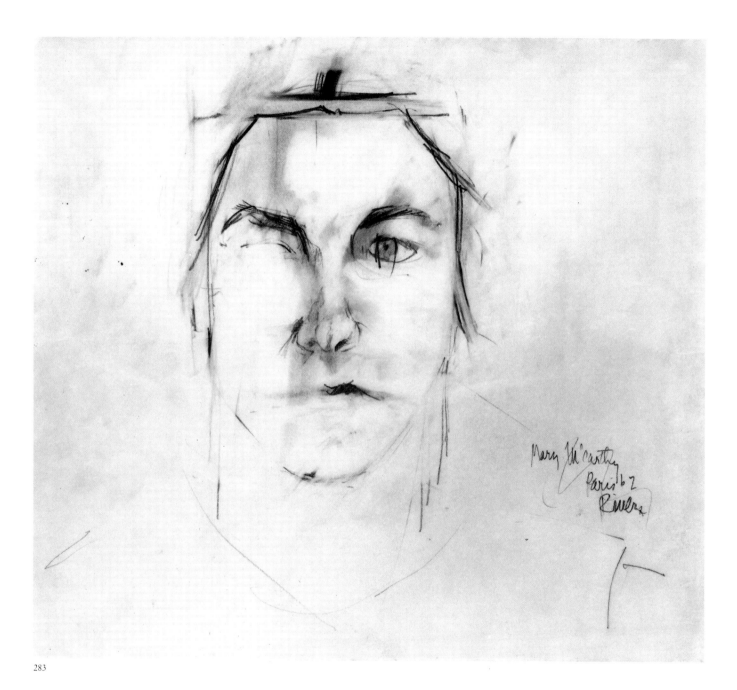

283

283. Portrait of Mary McCarthy
1962
Pencil on paper, 14½ x 16¼"
Collection Mr. and Mrs. Stanley S. Arkin, New York

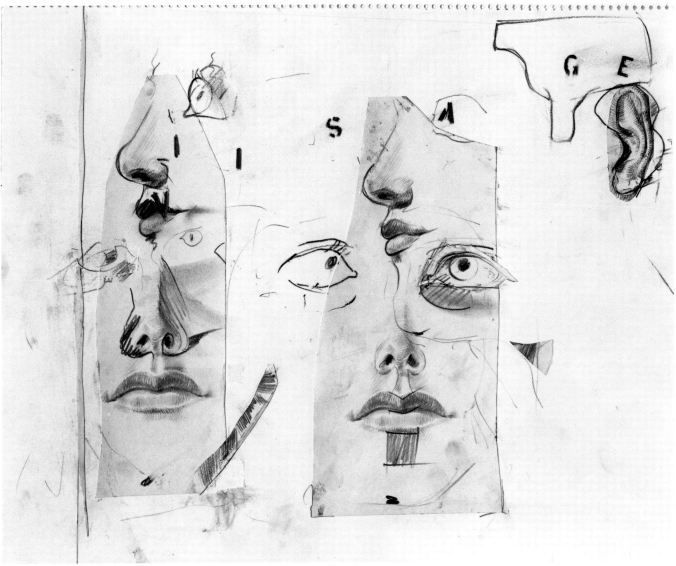

284

284. **How to Draw Series: Visage**
1963
Collage with pencil and charcoal on paper, 9¼ x 10⅜"
The Hirshhorn Museum and Sculpture Garden
Washington, D.C.

285. **Grey Webster**
1963
Pencil and crayon on paper, 9 x 9⅛"
Private collection

286. **Anemones**
1963
Pencil and colored papers on board, 9 x 10"
Collection Clarice Rivers, New York

287. **Bank Note**
1962
Pencil, 15¼ x 18½"
Collection Mr. and Mrs. Leonard Kasle
Franklin, Michigan

285

286

287

293

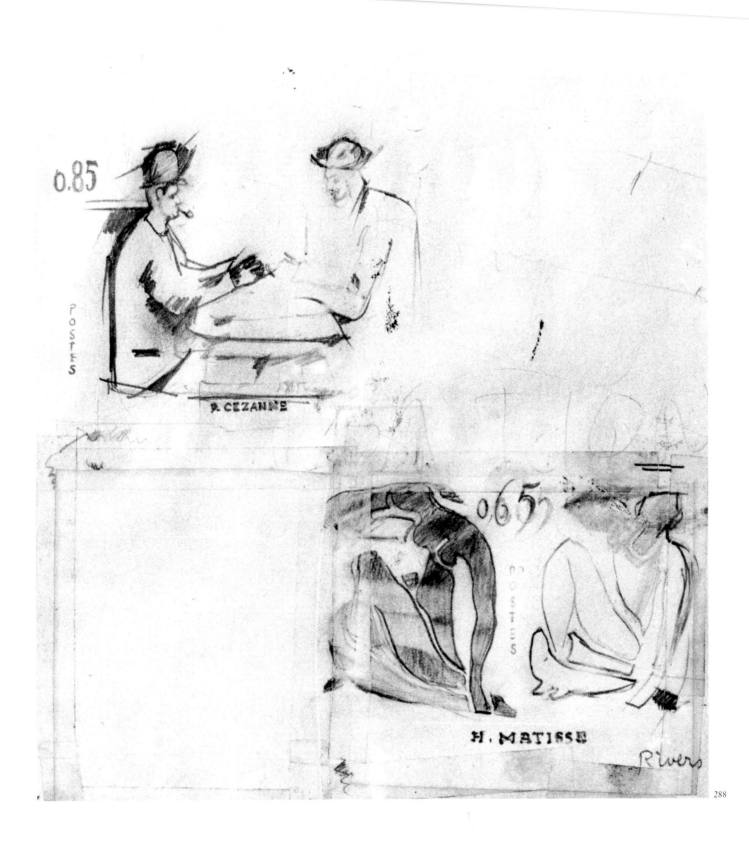

288

288. **French Postage Stamps**
1963
Pencil and collage, 10 x 9½"
Collection the artist

289. **De Kooning Drawing II**
1963
Pencil drawing, 13½ x 11½"
Collection Lester Avnet, New York

289

290. **Portrait of Imamu Baraka as Le Roi Jones**
1963
Pencil on paper, 14 x 16¾"
Private collection

290

Le Roi Jones

Larry Rivers

291. **Portrait of Ornette Coleman, Illustration of**
Firbank's New Rhythm—Auto
1962
Pencil and collage on paper, 14 x 16½"
Collection the artist

291

292

292. **Papa a Little Later**
1964
Pencil on paper, 18 x 18"
Collection Mr. and Mrs. Edward S. Gordon
New York

For Mama 1964
Larry Rivers

293

293. **Mama a Little Later**
1964
Pencil on paper, 18 x 18"
Collection Mr. and Mrs. Edward S. Gordon
New York

294

295

294. **Portrait of Le Roi Jones, Study for Poster for Two One-Act Plays The Toilet and The Slave**
1964
Crayon and photograph on board, relief, 15 x 12"
Private collection

295. **Negative Lion**
1964
Pencil, crayon and collage, 19 x 14¼"
Private collection

296. **Lions on Dreyfus Fund**
1964
Pencil, collage, and crayon, 23¼ x 17¼"
Private collection

297

297. **Head of Leonard Bernstein**
1965
Pencil on music paper, 14 x 16"
Collection Leonard Bernstein

298

298. **John Lindsay Collage**
1965
Pencil and crayon on board collage, 23½ x 22½″
Collection John M. Rodger, Jr., Cleveland, Ohio

299

300

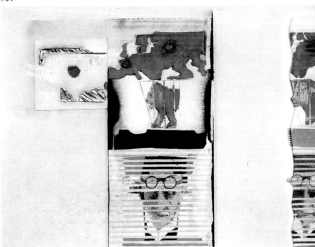

301

299. **Template, Horse, Butterflies and Birds**
1965
Mixed media with collage on wood, 14⅛ x 18″
Private collection

300. **Crows**
1965
Oil, crayon and pencil on board, 14⅛ x 16¾″
Collection the artist

301. **Stravinsky Collage**
1966
Collage with pencil, pastel and crayon, 12⅜ x 25½″
Svensk-Franska Konstgalleret, Stockholm, Sweden

302. **Drawing for Lamp Man Loves It**
Pencil, oil and collage on paper, 57¾ x 47″
Collection the artist

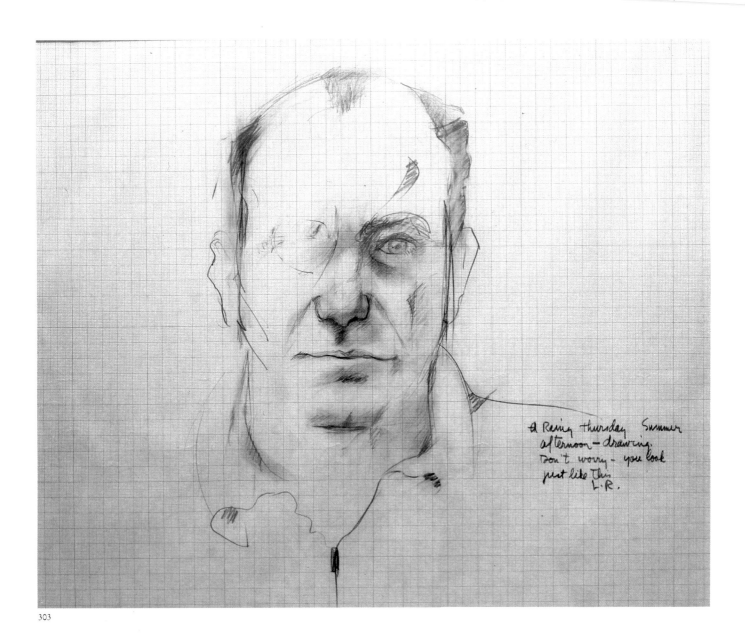

A Rainy thursday Summer
afternoon — drawing.
Don't worry — you look
just like this.
L·R.

303

303. **Portrait of Sam Hunter**
1965
Pencil on graph paper, 14 x 18″
Private collection

304

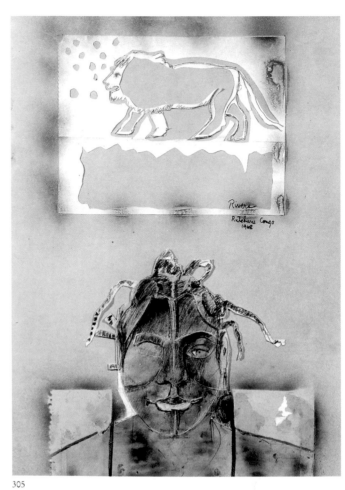

305

306

304. **Elimination of Nostalgia I**
1967
Crayon and pencil relief on board, 12 x 9¼″
Collection Mr. and Mrs. Marco de Laurenti, New York

305. **Congolese Woman and Lion**
1968
Pencil and collage, 24 x 18″
Private collection

306. **Janet Seated**
1968
Pencil, ballpoint, day-glo paper and collage, 24 x 18″
Private collection

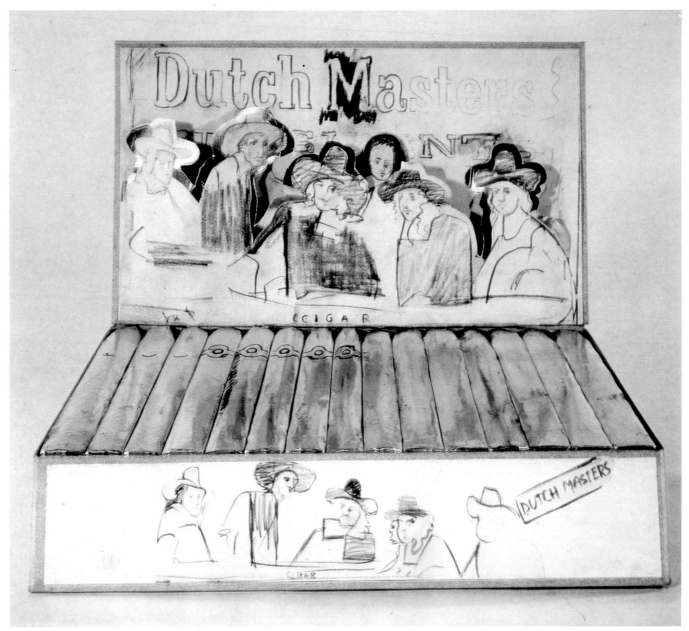

307

307. **Dutch Masters Silver**
1968
Construction with pencil, crayon, silverpaper
11¾ x 16 x 8¼″
Private collection

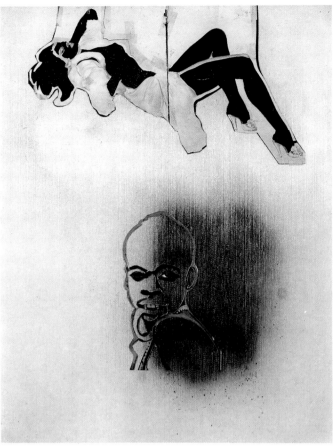

308

309

308. **Black is ·Black**
1968
Mixed media on pink pinstripe paper, 25⅜ x 20″
Private collection

309. **Snow Cap**
1970
Paper collage with pencil and colored crayon
encased in plastic, 17 x 14″
Private collection

310

310. **Study for the Boston Massacre I**
1970
Colored pencil on posterboard, 32 x 40"
Private collection

311

311. **Tryout for Boston Massacre** (three soldiers,
one mounted, with banners)
1970
Colored pencil on posterboard, 32 x 40″
Collection the artist

312

312. **Portrait of Aladar as a Hollow Column**
1971
Pencil and tape on paper in plastic, 14 x 16″
Collection Aladar Marberger, New York

313. **Self Portrait**
1972
Pencil with polaroid photograph, 39½ x 50″
Collection Earl McGrath, Los Angeles, California

313

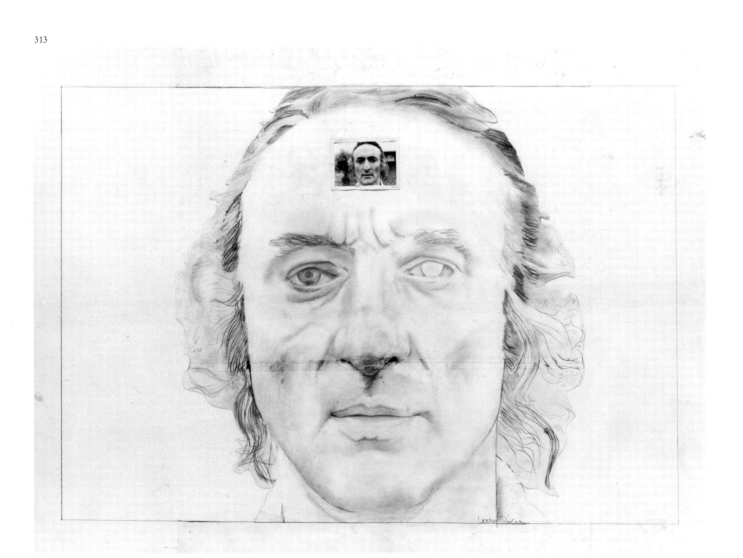

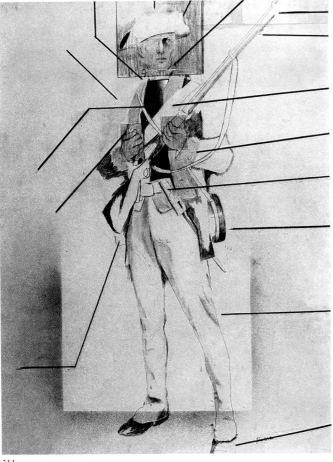

314

314. **Study after the Boston Massacre III**
1970
Colored pencil and cutout on posterboard, 40 x 32"
Collection the artist

315. **Mr. Steel (Leonard Kasle)**
1971
Collage encased in red plastic, 14 x 17"
Collection Mr. and Mrs. Leonard Kasle
Franklin, Michigan

316. **Dutch Masters VF**
1971
Paper collage with charcoal and colored pencil,
encased in plastic, 9¼ x 14¾"
Private collection

315

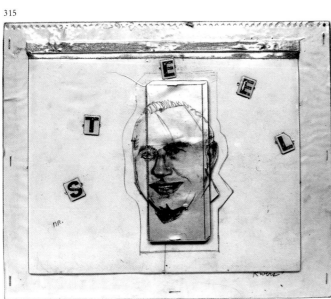

316

317

318

317. **Kinko and the Carp**
1974
Pencil on paper, 40 x 56"
Private collection

318. **Portrait of Miss Oregon I**
1973
Mixed media on paper, 66 x 108"
Collection Leonard Holzer, New York

319

320

319. **Utamaro's Courtesans**
1974
Pencil and colored pencil on paper, 81½ x 70″
Collection Killy Myers, New York

320. **Working Drawing for "Shushui's Erotic Art"**
1974
Pencil and colored pencil on tracing paper, 54 x 80¼″
Private collection

321

321. **Working Drawing of Hero for "Heroes of Chushingura"**
1974
Pencil and colored pencil on tracing paper
80½ x 54″
Private collection

322. **For C's 35th**
1974
Colored pencil on paper, 14 x 17″
Collection Clarice Rivers, New York

323. **Portrait of Sheila**
1975
Pencil on paper
Private collection

322

323

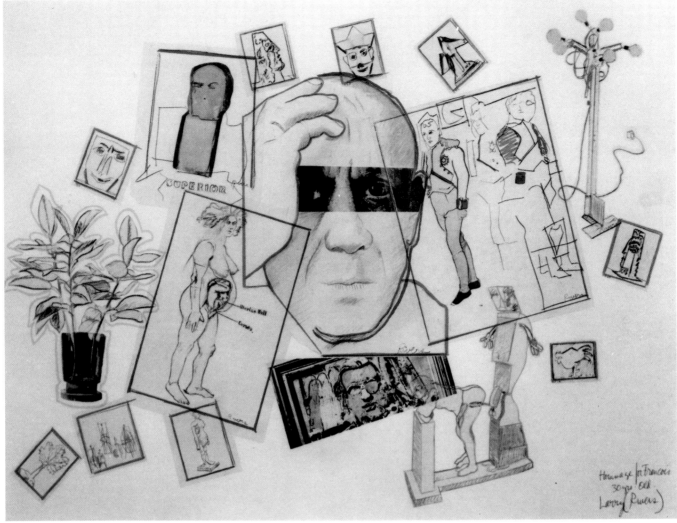

324

324. **Homage to Picasso**
1974
Pencil, photograph collage, 22 x 30¼″
Collection the artist

325

325. The Stripe is in the Eye of the Beholder:
Portrait of Barnett Newman
1975
Pencil on paper, 35¾ x 100½″
Collection Mr. David Pincus, New York

326

326. **Joe Glazer Sings Garbage**
1977
Collage with pencil, 18¼ x 18⅛"
Private collection

327

327. Two Lines of the Depression
1975
Pencil and colored pencil on paper, 84 x 84″
Marlborough Gallery, New York

328. **Nigeria Yesterday and Today Carbon Color**
1976
Pencil and carbon paper, 25½ x 40"
Private collection

329. **Burundi Stamps Carbon Color**
1976
Pencil and carbon paper, 25⅝ x 36⅝"
Collection the artist

330. **French Camel Carbon Color**
1976
Pencil and carbon paper, 36 x 46½"
Private collection

331. **Discontinued French Money**
1976
Pencil on paper collage, 27¼ x 37¾"
Collection the artist

328

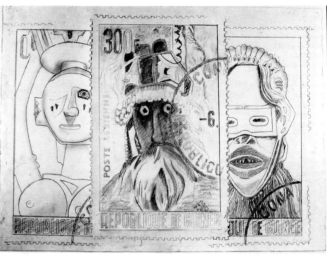

329

331

330

332

333

332. **Gwynne and Emma Rivers, Carbon Drawing**
1976
Colored carbon on paper, 23½ x 33¼″
Collection Susan Lloyd, Paris

333. **Reclining Figure**
1977
Pencil on paper, 10¾ x 14¾″
Private collection

334

334. **Scale Drawing for Rainbow Rembrandt's**
1977
Pencil on colored carbon and paper, 65 x 75½″
The Hirshhorn Museum and Sculpture Garden
Washington, D.C.

335

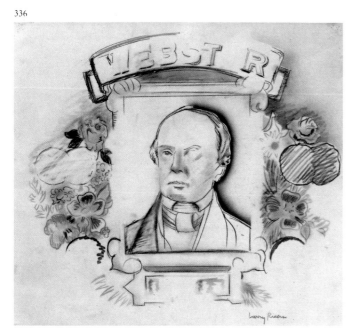

335. **Two Camels**
1978
Pencil and colored pencil on acetate, 15 x 21½"
Private collection

336. **Webster**
1978
Pencil, colored pencil and acrylic on paper, 26 x 30½"
Private collection

337. **Golden Oldies: Camels**
1978
Pencil and pastel on paper, 64 x 54"
Collection Ron Seff, New York

338

339

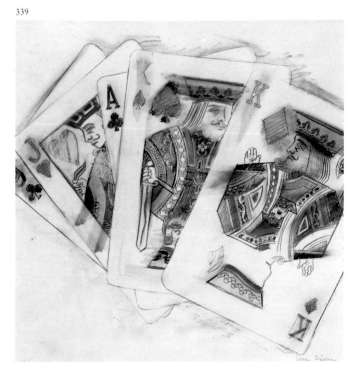

338. **Ace of Spades**
1978
Black pencil on acetate, 27½ x 24″
Private collection

339. **Pair of Kings**
1978
Pencil and colored pencil on paper, 24½ x 25″
Private collection

340. **Dying and Dead Veteran**
1978
Acrylic and charcoal on paper, 71 x 59″
Private collection

340

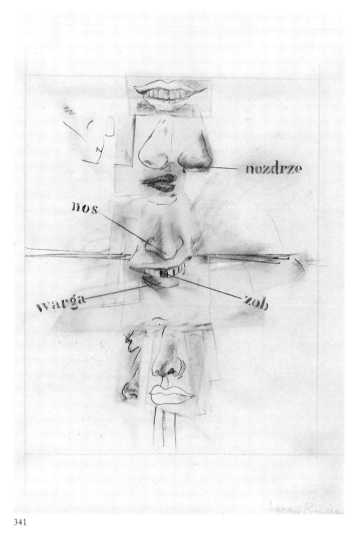

341

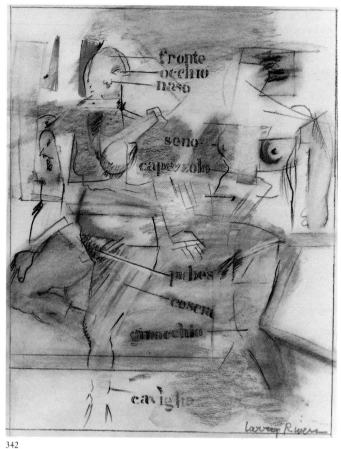

342

341. **Polish Vocabulary Lesson**
1978
Acrylic, pencil and colored pencil on paper, 18½ x 13¾″
Private collection

342. **Italian Vocabulary Lesson**
1978
Pencil and colored pencil on paper, 17½ x 14″
Private collection

343

343. **Study for "Chinese Information-Travel"**
1980
Charcoal, colored pencil and collage on paper
30¼ x 35¼"
Collection the artist

345

346

344. **Go Go and Camels**
     1978
     Colored pencil and acrylic on canvas, 60 x 40″
     Private collection

345. **The Continuing Interest in Abstract Art: Graduation**
     1981
     Pencil on paper mounted on canvas, 25½ x 34″
     Collection the artist

346. **Webster on Hand-Made Paper**
     1979
     Pencil and colored pencil on paper, 13¾ x 17″
     Private collection

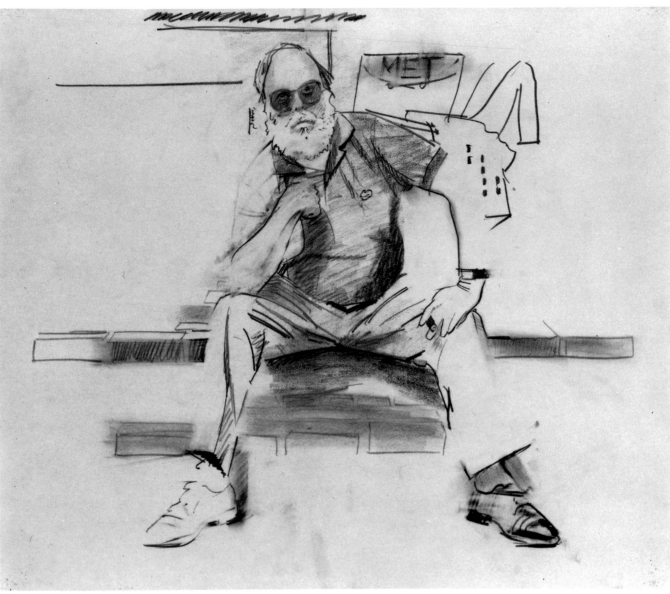

347

347. **Posing (Henry Geldzahler)**
1981
Pencil and colored pencil on paper, 23½ x 28″
Private collection

348. **The Continuing Interest in Abstract Art:
Frank and Susan in 1967**
1981
Relief, 39⅞ x 31⅛″
Collection the artist

page 336
349. **In the Artist's Studio Vertical**
1981
Pencil, colored pencil and tape on paper, 33⅜ x 23½″
Private collection

page 337
350. **Portrait of Mayor Koch**
1985
Pencil on paper
Private collection

349

350

351

351. **For the Magician of Lublin**
1983
Pencil and colored pencil mounted on canvas
17¼ x 19⅝"
Collection the artist

352 **Primo Levi: Witness Drawing**
1988
Pencil and pastel on paper, 26½ x 28½″
Collection the artist

BIOGRAPHY

1925 Born August 17 in The Bronx, New York, to Samuel and Sonya Grossberg.

1940 Began career as a jazz saxophonist, and changed his name to Larry Rivers.

1942 Enlisted in the U.S. Army Air Corps.

1943 Honorable discharge from the armed forces for medical reasons. Resumed career as a musician.

1944 Studied music theory and composition at the Juilliard School of Music, New York. First exposure to art when a jazz musician showed him a painting of a bass fiddle by Georges Braque.

1945 Began painting at Old Orchard Beach, Maine. Married Augusta Burger. Son Steven born.

1946 Separated from Augusta. Moved to Manhattan. Began to meet painters, poets and dancers.

1947 Enrolled in Hans Hofmann's school of painting in New York and Provincetown.

1948 Enrolled at New York University as an art education major.

1949 First one-man exhibition.

1950 First trip to Europe, spending eight months in Paris writing poetry. On returning to New York began painting full time living with mother-in-law Bertha "Berdie" Burger and sons Joseph and Steven.

1951 Graduated B.A. in Art Education from New York University. First of eleven annual solo exhibitions (except 1955) at Tibor de Nagy Gallery, organized by representative John Bernard Myers. Began sculpting in plaster.

1952 Designed sets for the play "Try! Try!" by Frank O'Hara, produced for the Artists' Theater by John Bernard Myers.

1953 Completed *Washington Crossing the Delaware*. Moved to Southampton, Long Island.

1954 First exhibition of sculpture. First painting acquisition (*The Burial*, by the Gloria Vanderbilt Foundation).

1955 First major museum acquisition (*Washington Crossing the Delaware*, by the Museum of Modern Art). Won third prize in the Corcoran Gallery national painting competition, for *Self-Figure*.

1956 One of twelve artists representing America at the "IV Bienal do Museu de Arte Moderna de Sao Paulo," Sao Paulo, Brazil.

1957 Mother-in-law Berdie Burger died at age 66. Began sculpting in welded metal. Began collaborating with Frank O'Hara on *Stones*, a series of lithographs of illustrated poetry. Won $32,000 on TV show "The $64,000 Question."

1958 Spent a month in Paris playing around town in several jazz bands.

1959 Having gone to Cedar Tavern for many years, comes away with a poem wrapped in a Cedar Bar Menu. Instead of illustrating the poem (his original intention), painted *Cedar Bar Menu I*. Seagram's Building purchased *Me II*.

1960 Began collaboration with Kenneth Koch on painting-poems.

1961 Married Clarice Price. Painted in a studio in Impasse Ronsin, Paris, where he met, became friends and collaborated with Jean Tinguely.

1962 The first Rivers-Tinguely collaboration, *The Friendship of America and France*, was shown at the Musee des Arts Decoratifs, Paris. London's Tate Gallery purchases *Parts of the Face: French Vocabulary Lesson*.

1963 Completed the commissioned *First New York Film Festival Billboard*.

1964 Traveled to Europe and North Africa. Informal artist-in-residence at the Slade School of Fine Arts, London, from January to June. Daughter Gwynne born.

1965 First comprehensive retrospective exhibition, of 170 paintings, drawings, sculptures and prints, organized by Sam Hunter, toured five U.S. museums. Prepared *The History of The Russian Revolution: From Marx to Mayakovsky* for inclusion in the final exhibition at the Jewish Museum.

1966 Designed sets and costumes for Stravinsky's *Oedipus Rex*, with the New York Philharmonic under Lukas Foss. Death of intimate friend and collaborator Frank O'Hara. Daughter Emma born. Winter of 1966-67 spent in London.

1967 Traveled to Central America to film the television documentary *Africa and I* with Pierre Gaisseau. Participated in the Museum of Modern Art's memorial exhibition for the late poet and curator Frank O'Hara.

1968 Returned to Africa with Gaisseau to complete documentary film. Narrowly escaped execution as a suspected mercenary. Completed giant two-part *Boston Massacre* murals for the New England Merchants National Bank of Boston.

1969 Separated from Clarice Price. Completed *Forty Feet of Fashion* for the Smithhaven Mall. Began working with spray cans.

1970 Completed *Some American History* for the De Menil Foundation, receiving highest price ever paid for a commissioned work. In a natural progression, working with spray cans led to airbrush painting and the use of acrylics. Began working with videotape.

1971 Traveled through Oregon and California.

1972 Returned to California and taped video segments for an operatic treatment of Kenneth Koch's poem "The Artist," which was performed at the Whitney Museum, New York. Taught at the University of California at Santa Barbara.

1973 Traveled to Sweden for group show at the Swedish Museum of Modern Art, Stockholm, where his work *Living at the Movies* was exhibited. Began series of paintings based on "The Coloring Book of Japan."

1974 Completed the Japanese series, shown at Marlborough Gallery.

1975 Traveled to Africa, where he made a short videotape with Peter Beard.

1976 Traveled to Russia at the invitation of the Union of Soviet Artists, where he lectured in several cities on contemporary American art. Made videotapes along the way.

1977 Began using color carbon. Began a series of works based on Rembrandt's *Polish Rider,* of which *Rainbow Rembrandt* was purchased by the Hirshhorn Museum.

1978 Began the *Golden Oldies* series, turning his characteristic historical approach to his own works of the 50s and 60s. Part of the series shown at ACA Galleries.

1980 Retrospective exhibition: Museo de Arte Contemporáneo de Caracas.

1980-81 Traveling retrospective exhibition:
Kestner-Gesellschaft, Hannover
Kunstverein, Munich
Kunsthalle, Tubingen
Staatliche Kunsthalle, Berlin

1981 Began living with artist Daria Deshuk.

1982 *The Continuing Interest in Abstract Art* series shown at F.I.C.A. (Grand Palais, Paris), Marlborough Fine Art (London) Ltd., and Marlborough Gallery, New York.

1983 Thirty-year survey at Guild Hall Museum, East Hampton, New York and Lowe Art Museum, Coral Gables, Florida.

1984 The mural *Philadelphia Now and Then* inaugurated at J.C. Penney, Philadelphia.

1984-85 *History of Matzoh: The Story of Jews* exhibited at The Jewish Museum, New York.

1985 Son Sam Deshuk Rivers born.

1986 Completed a computer art project for the BBC, London, to be seen on U.S. television. Prepared for an October one-man exhibition of new relief paintings at Marlborough Gallery, New York. Interest in the motif of dancers for the *Make Believe Ballroom* series, based originally on Fred Astaire and Ginger Rogers, continues, with the portrayals of other dancers, including modern dancer Merce Cunningham. Produced a commissioned cover for *The New York Times Magazine, Erasing the Past,* using concentration camp imagery. Research for this led to an interest in the Holocaust and the writings of Primo Levi, resulting in a set of large portraits of Levi.

1987 Early in the year traveled to the Dominican Republic in the hope of "working long hours and quietly" on *Umber Blues.* Reviews Ron Sukenik's book *"Down & In"* for the New York Times. Asked by the Philadelphia Historical Society to make a print celebrating the Bicentennial of the Constitution. Contributes a special eight-page project to *Artforum* (No. XXVI, No. 3, November 1987) "1000 Avant-Garde Plays" by Kenneth Koch. A concomitant interest in Duchamp and the modernist avant-garde leads to a cover design for the "Art at the Armory" catalogue based on Duchamp's *Nude Descending a Staircase.*

1988 Begins a series of large versions of Duchamp's *Nude Descending a Staircase,* with the title *75 Years Later.* Spoleto Festival U.S.A. exhibition at the Gibbs Art Gallery, Charleston, South Carolina.

ONE-MAN EXHIBITIONS

1949	Jane Street Gallery, New York	**1978**	ACA Galleries, New York
1951	Tibor de Nagy Gallery, New York	**1979**	Marlborough Gallery, New York
1952	Tibor de Nagy Gallery, New York	**1980**	Museo de Arte Contemporáneo de Caracas
1953	Tibor de Nagy Gallery, New York	**1980-82**	Traveling retrospective exhibition:
1954	Stable Gallery, New York (sculpture)		Kestner-Gesellschaft, Hannover

1949   Jane Street Gallery, New York
1951   Tibor de Nagy Gallery, New York
1952   Tibor de Nagy Gallery, New York
1953   Tibor de Nagy Gallery, New York
1954   Stable Gallery, New York (sculpture)
        Tibor de Nagy Gallery, New York
1956-60 Tibor de Nagy Gallery
1961   Martha Jackson Gallery, New York (sculpture)
        Tibor de Nagy Gallery, New York
        Dwan Gallery, Los Angeles
1962   Tibor de Nagy Gallery, New York
        Gimpel Fils, London
        Galerie Rive Droite, Paris
1963   Dwan Gallery, Los Angeles
1964   Gimpel Fils, London
1965-66 Traveling retrospective exhibition:
        Rose Art Museum, Brandeis University,
        Waltham, Mass.
        Pasadena Art Museum
        The Jewish Museum, New York
        The Detroit Institute of Arts
        The Minneapolis Institute of Arts
1970   The Art Institute of Chicago (drawings)
1970-71 Marlborough Gallery, New York
1973   Marlborough Gallery, New York
1973-74 Palais des Beaux-Arts, Brussels
1974-75 Marlborough Gallery, New York
1976   Gimpel Fils, London
1977   Marlborough Gallery, New York
        Robert Miller Gallery, New York
        Gimpel Fils, London

1978   ACA Galleries, New York
1979   Marlborough Gallery, New York
1980   Museo de Arte Contemporáneo de Caracas
1980-82 Traveling retrospective exhibition:
        Kestner-Gesellschaft, Hannover
        Kunstverein, Munich
        Kunsthalle, Tubingen
        Staatliche Kunsthalle, Berlin
1981   F.I.C.A., Paris
        Marlborough Fine Art (London) Ltd.
1982   Marlborough Gallery, New York
        Studio Marconi, Milan
1983   Elaine Horwich Gallery, Phoenix, Arizona
        Guild Hall Museum, East Hampton, New York
        Lowe Art Museum, Coral Gables, Florida
1984   Kouros Gallery, New York
1984-85 The Jewish Museum, New York
1985   Museum of the University of Pennsylvania,
        Philadelphia
1985-86 Marlborough Fine Art Ltd., Tokyo
1986   Adelphi University Center, Garden City,
        New York
        Jan Turner Gallery, Los Angeles, California
        Heland-Thorden-Wetterling Gallery,
        Stockholm, Sweden
        Marlborough Gallery, New York
1987   Simms Fine Art, New Orleans, Louisiana
1988   Spoleto Festival U.S.A., Gibbes Art Gallery,
        Charleston, South Carolina

PUBLIC COLLECTIONS

Allentown, PA: Allentown Art Museum
Baltimore, MD: The Baltimore Museum of Art
Boston, MA: New England Merchants National Bank
Buffalo, NY: Albright-Knox Gallery
Chicago, IL: The Art Institute of Chicago
      Container Corporation of America
Dallas, TX: Dallas Museum of Art
Easthampton, NY: Guild Hall
Fort Wayne, IN: Fort Wayne Museum of Art
Greensboro, NC: Weatherspoon Gallery of Art,
      University of North Carolina
Houston, TX: De Menil Foundation
Kansas City, MO: The Nelson-Atkins Museum of Art
Lawrence, KS: Spencer Museum of Art
Los Angeles, CA: Los Angeles County Museum of Art
Minneapolis, MN: The Minneapolis Institute of Art
New York, NY: The Solomon R. Guggenheim Museum
      The Metropolitan Museum of Art
      The Museum of Modern Art
      Joseph H. Seagram & Sons, Inc.

      Singer Company
      Whitney Museum of American Art
Norfolk, VA: The Chrysler Museum
Providence, RI: Museum of Art, Rhode Island School
      of Design
Raleigh, NC: North Carolina Museum of Art
San Francisco, CA: San Francisco Museum of Modern Art
Southampton, NY: The Parrish Art Museum
Utica, NY: Munson-Williams-Proctor Institute of Modern
      Art
Waltham, MA: Rose Art Museum, Brandeis University
Washington, DC: The Corcoran Gallery of Art
      The Hirshhorn Museum and Sculpture Garden
      National Gallery of Art
Caracas: Museo de Arte Contemporáneo
Cuenca, Spain: Museo de Arte Abstracto
London: Tate Gallery
Mexico City: Museo Rufino Tamayo
Stockholm: Svenske-Franska Konstgalliert

PLATE SECTIONS

I. **The Burial**
1952
Oil on Canvas, 60 x 108"
Fort Wayne Art School and Museum Fort Wayne,
Indiana

II. **Washington Crossing the Delaware**
1953
Oil on canvas, 83⅜ x 111⅛"
The Museum of Modern Art, New York,
given anonymously

III. **O'Hara**
1954
Oil on canvas, 97 x 53"
Collection the artist

IV. **Berdie Seated**
1953
Pencil on paper 8⅝ x 12"
Collection the artist

V. **Portrait of Berdie**
1954
Oil on canvas, 80¾ x 54⅜"
Museum of Art, Rhode Island School of Design
Providence

VI. **Double Portrait of Berdie**
1955
Oil on canvas, 70¾ x 82½"
Whitney Museum of American Art New York

VII. **Frank O'Hara with Hammer**
1955
Pencil on paper, 14 x 16½"
Collection the artist

VIII. **DeKooning with My Texas Hat**
1963
Pencil, crayon, cellophane tape on paper, 14 x 16⅞"
The Hirshhorn Museum and Sculpture Garden
Washington, D.C.

IX. **Joseph**
1954
Oil on canvas, 52½ x 45½"
Collection Frank M. Purnell, New York

X. **The Twenty-Five Cent Summer Cap**
1956
Oil on canvas, 53½ x 47"
The Hirshhorn Museum and Sculpture Garden
Washington, D.C.

XI. **The Studio**
1956
Oil on canvas, 82½ x 193½"
The Minneapolis Institute of Arts
Minneapolis, Minnesota

XII. **Dying and Dead Veteran**
1961
Oil on canvas, 70 x 94"
Private collection

XIII. **The Last Civil War Veteran**
1960
Oil on board, 10 x 8"
Private collection

XIV. **Buick Painting with P**
1960, Oil on canvas
48 x 61"
Collection Mr. and Mrs. Frank Titelman
Atlanta, Georgia

XV. **Parts of the Body**
(French and Italian Vocabulary)
1963
Oil and collage on board, 51½ x 40"
Collection the artist

XVI. **Clarice Pregnant**
1964
Pencil, 60 x 40"
Collection the artist

XVII. **The Elimination of Nostalgia A, B, C**
1967
Mixed media, 84 x 64½ x 25¾"
Collection Mr. and Mrs. Kent Klineman, New York

XVIII. **Double French Money**
1962
Oil on canvas, 72 x 60"
Collection Mr. and Mrs. Charles B. Benenson
Scarsdale, New York

XIX. **The History of the Russian Revolution:**
From Marx to Mayakovsky
1965
Mixed media construction, 53 pieces
14'4" x 32'5" x 18"
The Hirshhorn Museum and Sculpture Garden
Washington, D.C.

XX. **Golden Oldies 60s**
1978
Oil on canvas, 106 x 144"
Collection Sivia and Jeffrey H. Loria, New York

XXI. **History of Matzoh**
The Story of the Jews Part I
1982 (detail)
Private collection

XXII. **Public and Private**
1984-85
Oil on canvas, mounted on foamcore, 115 x 177"
Australian National Gallery, Canberra, Australia

XXIII. **A Vanished World: Trnava, Czecholsovakia, 1936**
Raising Geese I
1987
Oil on canvas, mounted on foamcore, 65½ x 60 x 5"
Private collection

XXIV **Berdie with American Flag**
1957
Oil on canvas, 20 x 25⅞"
The Nelson Gallery-Atkins Museum
Kansas City, Missouri

XXV. **Europe II**
1956
Oil on canvas, 54 x 48"
Collection Mr. and Mrs. Donald Weisberger
New York

XXVI. **From Public and Private: Fred Astaire**
1984
Pastel and pencil on paper, 20¼ x 27⅛"
Collection the artist

XXVII. **Primo Levi (Double Head) II**
1988
Oil on canvas, mounted on sculpted foamcore
73 x 58½ x 4"
Collection the artist

XXVIII. **Wedding Photo (Apart)**
1978-79
Pencil on paper, 29 x 36"
Collection the artist

COLOR PLATES

1. **Studio Interior**
1948
Oil on paper, 17½ x 23½"
Collection of Gloria and Dan Stern, New York

2. **Portrait of Frank O'Hara**
1953
Oil on canvas, 54 x 40"
Collection the artist

3. **The Family**
1954-55
Oil on canvas, 82 x 72"
Collection Dr. Alvin Wesley, New York

4. **Augusta**
1954
Oil on canvas, 83 x 53"
Collection the artist

5. **Boy in Blue Denim** (Portrait of Steven)
1955
Oil on canvas, 53½ x 38"
The Parrish Art Museum, Southampton, New York

6. **Europe I**
1956
Oil on canvas, 72 x 48"
The Minneapolis Institute of Arts
Anonymous gift

7. **The Journey**
1956
Oil on canvas, 104 x 115"
Collection the artist

8. **Molly and Breakfast**
1956
Oil on canvas, 48 x 72"
The Hirshhorn Museum and Sculpture Garden
Washington, D.C.

9. **The Accident**
1957
Oil on canvas, 84 x 90"
Collection Joseph E. Seagram & Sons, Inc.
New York

10. **The Pool**
1956
Oil, charcoal, and bronze paint on canvas
8'7⅜" x 7'8⅜"
The Museum of Modern Art, New York.
Gift of Mr. & Mrs. Donald Weisberger

11. **It's Raining Anita Huffington**
1957
Oil on canvas, 104 x 115"
Collection the artist

12. **Drugstore I**
1959
Oil on canvas, 85 x 66"
Collection Mr. Barry Benedak, Baltimore, Maryland

13. **Blue: The Byzantine Empress**
1958
Oil on canvas, 72 x 60"
Collection Mrs. Albert M. Greenfield
Philadelphia, Pennsylvania

14. **Me in a Rectangle**
1959
Oil on canvas, 65¾ x 48¾"
Neuberger Museum, State University of
New York at Purchase
Gift of Jane and Jay Braus

15. **Cedar Bar Menu I**
1959
Oil on canvas, 47½ x 35"
Collection the artist

16. **U.N. Painting**
1959
Oil on canvas, 96 x 96"
Marisa del Re Gallery, New York

17. **The Next to Last Confederate**
1959
Oil on canvas, 60 x 46"
Collection Mr. and Mrs. Guy Weill
Scarsdale, New York

18. **The Last Civil War Veteran**
1959
Oil and charcoal on canvas, 82½ x 64½"
The Museum of Modern Art, New York
Blanchette Rockefeller Fund

19. **Final Veteran**
1960
Oil on canvas, 78¾ x 51"
Private collection

20. **Pink Tareyton**
1960
Oil on canvas, 12 x 9"
Collection the artist

21. **Pequeño as de espadas**
1960
Oil on canvas, 10 x 8"
Collection the artist

22. **Kings**
1960
Oil on canvas, 52 x 60″
Private collection
23. **Webster Flowers**
1961
Oil on canvas, 60 x 72″
The Hirshhorn Museum and Sculpture Garden
Washington, D.C.
24. **Barmitzvah Photograph Painting**
1961
Oil on canvas, 72 x 60″
Collection George A.N. Schneider, New York
25. **Parts of the Face: French Vocabulary Lesson**
1961
Oil on canvas, 29½ x 29½″
The Tate Gallery, London
26. **Marriage Photograph**
1961
Oil on canvas, 71 x 98″
Private collection
27. **French Money Painting II**
1962
Oil and charcoal on linen, 35⅛ x 59″
The Hirshhorn Museum and Sculpture Garden
Washington, D.C.
28. **Italian Vocabulary Lesson**
1962
Oil on canvas, 30 x 24″
Private collection
29. **Amel Camel**
1962
Oil on canvas and collage, 39 x 39″
William College Museum of Art,
Williamstown, Massachusetts
30. **Friendship of America and France**
(Kennedy and DeGaulle)
1961-62, repainted 1970
Oil on canvas, 51½ x 76½″
Private collection
31. **I Like Ingres—A Copy**
1962
Oil on canvas, 60 x 42″
The Hirshhorn Museum and Sculpture Garden
Washington, D.C.
32. **Portrait of Joseph H. Hirshhorn**
1963
Oil on canvas, 71 x 48″
The Hirshhorn Museum and Sculpture Garden
Washington, D.C.
33. **Celebrating Shakespeare's 400th Birthday**
(Titus Andronicus)
1963
Oil on canvas, 58 x 77¾″
Private collection
34. **Mauve Dutch Master**
1963
Oil and collage, 25 x 26″
Private collection
35. **Dutch Masters I**
1963
Oil on canvas, 40 x 50″
Collection The Fine Arts Center,
Cheekwood, Nashville, Tennessee

36. **Dutch Masters and Cigars II**
1963
Oil and board collage on canvas, 96 x 67⅜″
The Harry N. Abrams Family Collection, New York
37. **Camels 6 x 4**
1962
Oil on canvas, 72 x 48″
Collection Mrs. J. Frederick Byers III, New York
38. **Africa II**
1962-63
Oil on canvas, 112¾ x 113″
Collection Helyn and Ralph Goldenberg
Chicago, Illinois
39. **Cézanne Stamp**
1963
Oil on canvas, 42 x 54″
The Hirshhorn Museum and Sculpture Gardeen
Washington, D.C.
40. **Eyes and Ears**
1963
Oil, pencil and paper collage on paper, 14¾ x 18″
Private collection
41. **Parts of the Body: English Vocabulary Lesson**
1963
Oil and collage on board, 60 x 40″
Richard Gray Gallery, Chicago
42. **Lions on the Dreyfus Fund III**
1964
Oil and collage with stencil cutouts on canvas
14½ x 78½″
The Art Institute of Chicago, Illinois
43. **The Greatest Homosexual**
1964
Oil and collage on canvas, 80 x 61″
The Hirshhorn Museum and Sculpture Garden
Washington, D.C.
44. **Polish Vocabulary Lesson**
1964
Oil on canvas, 24 x 30″
Private collection
45. **Jim Dine Storm Windows**
1965
Mixed media, 29 x 25 x 2¾″
Collection the artist
46. **Plexiglas Playmate**
1966
Mixed media, 62 x 49 x 15″
Collection Playboy Club, Chicago, Illinois
47. **Webster and Europe**
1967
Relief collage with crayon and charcoal, 18 x 20″
The Phoenix Art Museum, Phoenix, Arizona
(Gift of Mr. Edward Jacobson)
48. **The Boston Massacre** (detail)
1968
Acrylic and oil on canvas, 19′6″ x 14″ (full size)
Collection The New England Merchants National
Bank of Boston, Massachusetts
49. **Study for Last Civil War Veteran**
1970
Mixed media, 31¼ x 23½″
Private collection
50. **The Ghetto Stoop**
1969
Construction
13′6″ x 10′4″ x 8′10″
Menil Foundation, Houston, Texas

51. **America's Number One Problem**
1969
Electrified mixed media construction, 26½ x 20½ x 5″
Collection the artist

52. **I Like Olympia in Black Face**
1970
Mixed media construction, 71⅝ x 76⅜ x 39⅜″
Collection Musée National d'Art Moderne,
Centre Georges Pompidou, Paris

53. **Some American History: African Continent and African**
1970
Construction, 67 x 64 x 12½″
Menil Foundation, Houston Texas

54. **The Divers**
1968-72
Mixed media construction 96 x 70 x 7″
Collection the artist

55. **Heroes of Chushingura**
1974
Acrylic on canvas, 97 x 138″
Arnold Gallery, Atlanta, Georgia

56. **Kinko the Nymph Bringing Happy Tidings**
1974
Acrylic on canvas, 78 x 108″
The Gund Art Foundation
Cambridge, Massachusetts

57. **Utamaro's Women**
1975
Acrylic on canvas, 72¾ x 56¾″
Private collection

58. **Beauty and the Beast II**
1975
Pencil on paper, 70¾ x 778¼″
Collection Harry Horn, Nairobi

59. **Mixed Patriotic Stamps**
1976
Acrylic on canvas, 48 x 36″
Private collection

60. **Poem and Portrait: John Ashbery**
1977
Acrylic on canvas, 76 x 58″
Collection the artist

61. **Rainbow Rembrandt**
1977
Acrylic on canvas, 66 x 76″
Collection The Joseph H. Hirshhorn Museum
and Sculpture Garden, Washington, D.C.

62. **Rainbow Rembrandt II**
1977
Acrylic on canvas, 66 x 76″
Private collection

63. **Golden Oldies 50s**
1978
Oil and mixed media on canvas and plywood
106 x 144″
Private collection

64. **Golden Oldies: The Greatest Homosexual**
1978
Acrylic and colored pencil on paper, 86 x 56″
Collection Mr. David Sawyers
Stony Creek, Connecticut

65. **Graph Camel**
1978
Acrylic on canvas, 36 x 36″
Private collection

66. **Golden Oldies: French Vocabulary Lesson**
1978
Acrylic, pencil and colored pencil on paper
30¼ x 24¼″
Collection Mr. Simon Daro Dawidowicz
Miami Beach, Florida

67. **Portrait of Daniel Webster on a Flesh Field II**
1979
Acrylic on canvas, 74 x 80″
Virginia Museum of Fine Arts
Richmond, Virginia

68. **Wedding Photo** (On Approval)
1979
Acrylic on canvas, 38 x 44″
Sidney and Francis Lewis Foundation
Richmond, Virginia

69. **Beyond Camels**
1980
Acrylic on canvas, 98 x 79″
Private collection

70. **Front and Back Camel**
1980
Pastel and graphite on paper, 16½ x 25″
Private collection

71. **Golden Oldies: Dutch Masters**
1978
Charcoal and acrylic on paper, 89 x 57″
Collection Sivia and Jeffrey H. Loria, New York

72. **Syndics of the Drapery Guild as Dutch Masters**
1978-79
Acrylic on canvas and board, 98½ x 69½ x 5½″
Private collection

73. **Boucher's Punishment**
1981
Acrylic on canvas, 70 x 48½″
Collection the artist

74. **The Continuing Interest in Abstract Art: Cutting**
1981
Relief: pencil and colored pencil on paper, 30⅛ x 22¼″
Marlborough Gallery, New York

75. **The Continuing Interest in Abstract Art: From Photos of Gwynne and Emma Rivers**
1981
Mixed media, 78⅛ x 80¾″
Jan Turner Gallery, Los Angeles, California

76. **The Continuing Interest in Abstract Art: Letters from Jean Tinguely and Niki de Saint-Phalle**
1981
Acrylic on canvas, 78⅛ x 83⅜″
Collection the artist

77. **The Continuing Interest in Abstract Art: Tinguely's Letter**
1981
Relief, 29 x 27½″
Private collection

78. **The Continuing Interest in Abstract Art: Now and Then**
1981
Acrylic on canvas
76⅛ x 80½″
Collection Roland and Eleanor Miller, Courtesy
J.B. Speed Museum, Louisville, Kentucky

79. **The Continuing Interest in Abstract Art: on the Phone I**
1981
Acrylic on canvas, 52 x 77″
Van Straaten Gallery, Chicago, Illinois

80. **The Continuing Interest in Abstract Art:**
    Sketches with Self-Portrait
    1981
    Acrylic on canvas, 56 x 44″
    Private collection
81. **The Continuing Interest in Abstract Art: Sheila**
    1981
    Acrylic on canvas, 76⅛ x 80½″
    Collection Roland and Eleanor Miller, Courtesy
    J.B. Speed Museum, Louisville Kentucky
82. **The Continuing Interest in Abstract Art: Posing**
    1981
    Pencil and colored pencil, 28 x 21⅛″
    Private collection
83. **The Continuing Interest in Abstract Art:**
    The Collector
    1981
    Relief: Pencil and color pencil on paper
    42¼ x 29 x 2″
    Collection the artist
84. **Dear Dale**
    1973-82
    Oil on canvas, 70 x 83″
    Private collection
85. **History of Matzoh** (The Story of the Jews)
    Part II
    1983
    Oil on canvas, 120 x 168″
    Collection Sivia and Jeffrey H. Loria, New York
86. **History of Matzoh** (The Story of the Jews)
    Part II
    1983 (study)
    Private collection
87. **History of Matzoh** (The Story of the Jews)
    Part III
    1983
    Acrylic on canvas, 116¼ x 180″
    Collection Sivia and Jeffrey H. Loria, New York
88. **History of Matzoh** (The Story of the Jews)
    Part III
    1983 (study)
    Private collection
89. **Out**
    1983
    Pencil and colored pencil
    33¼ x 29¼″
    Private collection
90. **Bad Bird**
    1983
    Oil on canvas mounted on sculpted foamcore
    62 x 49″
    Collection the artist
91. **An Old Sicilian Story**
    1984
    Relief, oil on canvas mounted on sculpted foamcore
    79 x 116″
    Private collection
92. **From Picnic Photo**
    1985
    Oil on canvas mounted on sculpted foamcore
    58½ x 73″
    Private collection
93. **Cubism Today: Striped Face**
    1985
    Oil on canvas mounted on sculpted foamcore
    42 x 30¼″
    Collection Mr. and Mrs. Ben Frankel
    Philadelphia, Pennsylvania

94. **1924 and Matisse**
    1985
    Oil on canvas mounted on sculpted foamcore
    96 x 120″
    Elaine Horwitch Gallery, Santa Fe, New Mexico
95. **Desert Scene Relief**
    1985
    Mixed media, oil on canvas, relief on foamcore
    51 x 41″
    Heland Thorden Wetterling Galleries, New York
96. **Entwined Figures**
    1985
    Relief, oil on canvas, 50 x 65″
    Collection Sivia and Jeffrey H. Loria, New York
97. **Dutch Masters Box**
    1985
    Mixed media relief, paper and colored pencil on
    paper, mounted on sculpted foamcore, 82¾ x 57 x 21¼″
    Private collection
98. **The Peaceful Past**
    1985
    Colored pencil, 33 x 31″
    Private collection
99. **25 Birds of the Northeast**
    1985-86
    Oil on canvas mounted on sculpted foamcore
    58 x 80½″
    Simms Fine Art, New York
100. **Planned Parenthood**
    1986
    Oil on canvas mounted on sculpted foamcore
    100 x 80″
    Collection the artist
101. **Kinko the Nymph**
    1985-86
    Acrylic on canvas mounted on foamcore
    32 x 64 x 4″
    Collection The Gund Art Foundation
    Cambridge, Massachusetts
102. **Matisse Opera and the Continuous Line**
    1986
    Oil on canvas mounted on sculpted foamcore
    68 x 56″
    Collection Frederick Weisman Co.
    Baltimore, Maryland
103. **Chinese Information: Female Rider**
    1983-1986
    Oil on canvas mounted on sculpted foamcore
    36 x 36″
    Private collection
104. **Chinese Information: Male Rider**
    1983-1986
    Oil on canvas mounted on sculpted foamcore
    36 x 36″
    Jan Turner Gallery, Los Angeles, California
105. **Duck Farm Relief: Umber Pants**
    1986
    Oil on canvas mounted on sculpted foamcore
    47 x 42″
    Collection Mr. and Mrs. Myron Beigler
    Los Altos, California
106. **A Vanished World: Trnava, Czecholsovakia, 1936**
    Raising Geese I
    1987
    Oil on canvas, mounted on foamcore, 65½ x 60 x 5″
    Private collection

107. **Relief from Berdie Photo**
1986
Mixed media relief, 53 x 43"
Private collection

108. **Work and Portrait of Red Grooms**
1986
Oil on canvas mounted on sculpted foamcore
64 x 61"
Collection Mr. and Mrs. Robert Schniler
Boca Raton, Florida

109. **Back to Back I**
1986
Oil on canvas mounted on sculpted foamcore
34 x 48"
Collection Marcia Levine, New York

110. **Dancing with the Dancer, II**
1986
Oil on canvas, 28½ x 23"
Collection Mr. and Mrs. Sidney R. Onobskey
San Francisco, California

111. **Make Believe Ballroom, Rita's Red Dress**
1987
Oil on canvas mounted on sculpted foamcore
57¼ x 51 x 4"
Private collection

112. **Make Believe Ballroom: The Dip**
1987
Oil on canvas mounted on sculpted foamcore
60¾ x 65½"
Private collection

113. **A Song to the Avant-Garde I**
1987
Pencil and collage on paper, 10½ x 11"
Collection the artist

114. **A Song to the Avant-Garde II**
1987
Pencil and collage on paper, 10¼ x 10½"
Collection the artist

115. **A Song to the Avant-Garde III**
1987
Pencil and collage on paper, 10⅛ x 10½"
Collection the artist

116. **A song to the Avant-Garde IV**
1987
Pencil and collage on paper, 15¾ x 16⅛"
Collection the artist

117. **A Song to the Avant-Garde V**
1987
Pencil and collage on paper, 16 x 15⅝"
Collection the artist

118. **A song to the Avant-Garde VI**
1987
Pencil and collage on paper, 15¾ x 15⅞"
Collection the artist

119. **A Song to the Avant-Garde VII**
1987
Pencil and collage on paper, 15¾ x 15⅞"
Collection the artist

120. **A Song to the Avant-Garde VIII**
1987
Pencil and collage on paper, 15⅝ x 15¾"
Collection the artist

121. **Portrait of Paula Gordon**
1987
Oil on canvas mounted on sculpted foamcore
64 x 70¼"
Collection Mr. and Mrs. Edward Gordon, New York

122. **Last Civil War Veteran: Indigo Blue**
1987
Oil on canvas mounted on sculpted foamcore, 75¼ x 57½ x 5"
Collection the artist

123. **Portrait of Leonard Bernstein**
1987
Pastel and color pencil, 11 x 18"
Private collection

124. **Umber Blues II, Sonny on the Side Relief**
1987
Oil on canvas mounted on sculpted foamcore, 34 x 49"
Collection the artist

125. **Dick Schwartz, Umber Blues**
1987
Oil on canvas, 64½ x 79"
Private collection

126. **Daniel Webster Amidst the Cigar Box Paraphernalia**
1987
Acrylic on canvas, 74 x 80⅛"
Private collection

127. **Dancer in an Abstract Field: Merce Spreading I**
1988
Oil on canvas mounted on sculpted foamcore
33½ x 56½ x 2½"
Private collection

128. **Dancer in an Abstract Field: Merce Spreading II**
1988
Oil on canvas mounted on sculpted foamcore
33½ x 56½ x 2½"
Private collection

129. **Dancer in an Abstract Field: Susan Bending**
1988
Oil on canvas mounted on sculpted foamcore
39 x 45½ x 2½"
Private collection

130. **Dancer in an Abstract Field: Fred Twisting I**
1988
Oil on canvas mounted on sculpted foamcore
39½ x 43½"
Private collection

131. **Dancer in an Abstract Field: Fred Flying I**
1988
Oil on canvas mounted on sculpted foamcore
40¾ x 54¾ x 2½"
Private collection

132. **Seventy-Five Years Later: Naples**
1988
Oil on canvas mounted on sculpted foamcore
74¼ x 47½ x 3"
Private collection

133. **Seventy-Five Years Later: Indigo**
1988
Oil on canvas mounted on sculpted foamcore
71 x 44 x 4"
Collection Peter Lewis
Cleveland, Ohio

134. **Primo Levi I**
1988
Oil on canvas mounted on sculpted foamcore
73 x 58½ x 4"
Collection La Stampa, Turin, Italy

135. **Primo Levi: Witness**
1988
Oil on canvas mounted on sculpted foamcore
58½ x 33 x 4"
Collection La Stampa, Turin, Italy

BLACK & WHITE PLATES

136. **Football Players**
1951
Oil and collage, 42 x 47½"
Collection Mr. and Mrs Oscar L. Gerber
Highland Park, Illinois

137. **Reclining Female Figure**
Bronze, 6½ x 16"
Collection the artist

138. **Berdie**
1952
Bronze, 31½" high
Collection the artist

139. **Self-portrait**
1953
Pastel and black chalk, 28½ x 21"
Art Institute of Chicago, Illinois

140. **Self Figure**
1953
Oil on canvas, 93⅜ x 65½"
The Corcoran Gallery of Art, Washington, D.C.

141. **Female Nude and Floor**
1953
(restored, 1956)
Plaster and wood planks, 68" high
Collection the artist

142. **Head of a Man**
1953
Bronze, 16½ x 7 x 11"
Collection the artist

143. **Berdie in the Garden**
1954
Oil on canvas, 61¾ x 50¼"
Collection David Daniels, New York

144. **Woman with Cat**
1954
Oil on canvas
Private collection

145. **Double Portrait of John Myers**
1954
Bronze, 72" high with base
Collection David P. Bassine, New York

146. **Child with Dolls**
Oil on canvas
1956
24 x 18"
Collection the artist

147. **Southampton Backyard**
1956
Oil on canvas, 35⅜ x 40"
Private collection

148. **The Athlete's Dream**
1956
Oil on canvas, 82 x 128"
National Museum of American Art
Smithsonian Institution, Washington, D.C.

149. **Bedroom**
1955
Oil on canvas, 85 x 71½"
Collection Dr. Frank M. Purnell, New York

150. **Portrait of Dr. Kenneth Wright**
1956
Oil on canvas, 17½ x 20¾"
Collection Dorothy Wright
Southampton, New York

151. **Comic Collaboration with Kenneth Koch**
1956
Gouache and mixed media, 19 x 24"
Private collection

152. **Portrait of Betty Weisberger**
1957
Oil on canvas, 27½ x 35"
Collection Mr. and Mrs. Donald M. Weisberger
New York

153. **Jazz Musician**
1958
Oil on canvas, 70 x 58"
Private collection

154. **Iron Maiden (Ford Fenders)**
1957
Steel, 84" high
Collection the artist

155. **Kabuki in a Rectangle**
1957
Welded steel, 84" high
Whereabouts unknown

156. **The Wall**
1957
Oil on canvas, 32 x 44"
Collection Mrs. Lloyd H. Smith, New York

157. **Red Molly**
1957
Oil on canvas, 69 x 58"
Collection Mr. and Mrs. Selig S. Burrows
New York

158. **Untitled**
1958
Oil on canvas, 46 x 44¾"
Collection the artist

159. **Night Painting and Maxine**
1958
Oil and charcoal on linen, 72⅛ x 60¼"
The Hirshhorn Museum and Sculpture Garden
Washington, D.C.

160. **Summer 1958, Maxine**
1958
Oil on canvas, 24½ x 32"
Collection Mr. and Mrs. Guy Weill
Scarsdale, New York

161. **The Welding Wall**
1958
Oil on canvas, 71½ x 81½"
Collection Mr. and Mrs. Donald M. Weisberger
New York

162. **Pots and Pans**
1958
Oil on canvas, 47 x 41"
Collection Mr. and Mrs. I Nelson, New York

163. **The Drummer.**
1958
Oil on canvas, 68 x 58"
Collection Mr. and Mrs. Guy Weill, Scarsdale, New York

164. **Second Avenue with "The"**
1958
Oil on canvas, 72¾ x 82¾"
Collection Mr. and Mrs. Patrick B. McGinnis
Cincinnati, Ohio

165. **Miss New Jersey**
1959
Oil on canvas, 60 x 48"
Private collection

166. **Horses**
1959
Oil on canvas, 79 x 60″
Collection Stanley Bard, New York

167. **Jack of Spades**
1960
Oil on canvas, 24 x 18″
Collection the artist

168. **Cousin**
1960
Oil on canvas, 60 x 52″
Private collection

169. **Dougherty Ace of Spades**
1960
Oil on canvas, 74 x 56
Museum of Art, Fort Lauderdale, Florida

170. **Washington Crossing the Delaware II**
1960
Oil on canvas, 7 x 9′
Whitney Museum of American Art, New York

171. **New York, 1950-60**
(collaboration with Kenneth Koch)
1961
Oil on canvas, 69 x 84″
Private collection

172. **Disque Bleu**
1961
Oil on canvas, 13 x 13″
Collection the artist

173. **Turning Friendship of America and France**
1961
Oil on canvas with motorized stand, 26¾ x 17 x 11½″
Collection the artist

174. **Portrait of Howard Kanovitz**
1960
Oil on canvas on wood, 19¼ x 21¼″
Collection Arthur Paul, Chicago, Illinois

175. **Cedar Bar Menu II**
1961
Oil on canvas, 48¼ x 36″
Collection Mr. and Mrs. Richard Titelman
Atlanta, Georgia

176. **Marriage Photograph II**
1961
Oil on canvas, 77 x 60″
Collection the artist

177. **Mr. Art (Portrait of David Sylvester)**
1962
Oil on canvas, 72 x 52″
Private collection

178. **Eight of Clubs**
1961
Oil and charcoal on canvas, 10⅛ x 8⅛″
Collection the artist

179. **Parts of the Face: French**
1961
Oil board on relief, 11¼ x 11¼″
Private collection

180. **Study for Civil War Veteran, Dead**
1961
Collage and pencil, paint and assorted papers
17 x 14″
Collection Mr. and Mrs. Marco di Laurenti
New York

181. **Parts of the Body: French Vocabulary Lesson**
1961-62
Oil on canvas, 72 x 48″
Private collection

182. **Parts of the Body**
(French and Italian Vocabulary)
1963
Oil and collage on board, 51½ x 40″
Collection the artist

183. **Typewriter Painting**
1962
Oil on canvas, 57½ x 45″
Private collection

184. **Yeux: Parts of the Face**
1962
Oil and collage on canvas
Private collection

185. **First New York Film Festival Billboard**
1963
Oil on canvas, 9′6″ x 15′
The Hirshhorn Museum and Sculpture Garden
Washington, D.C.

186. **Portrait of Dr. Bernard Brodsky**
1963
Oil on canvas, 65 x 48″
Collection Dr. and Mrs. Bernard Brodsky, New York

187. **Dutch Masters, Presidents**
1963
Oil on board and collage, 30 x 35½″
Private collection

188. **Barbara Goldsmith: Echoes and Parts**
1963
Oil and collage on canvas, 68 x 80″
Collection C. Gerald Goldsmith, New York

189. **Moon Man and Moon Lady**
1963
Oil on canvas, 46 x 68″
Private collection

190. **Here Lies Shakespeare**
1963
Oil and collage on board, 60 x 40″
Private collection

191. **Window Webster**
1963
Collage on board, 60 x 40″
Collection the artist

192. **The Greeks**
1963
Bronze, h. 132″
Collection the artist

193. **Notes**
1964
Mixed media, 38¾ x 30¼″
Private collection

194. **Dutch Masters Presidents Relief**
1964
Oil and collage on canvas mounted on wood box
98 x 69½ x 12″
Private collection

195. **Dutch Masters Relief**
1964
Oil and collage on board, mounted on wood
32⅜ x 26 x 7¾″
Private collection

196. **Dutch Masters (Corona)**
1964
Oil and collage on canvas, 35½ x 25″
Collection Jacques Kaplan, New York
197. **Parts of the Body: English Vocabulary Lesson**
1964
Plaster and steel, 83¾ x 90½ x 24¼″
Collection the artist
198. **Electric Webster**
1964
Oil, plexiglas, collage and electric light, 30 x 44″
Collection Jacques Kaplan, New York
199. **The Identification Manual** (closed)
1964
Oil and collage on canvas, 47 x 30″
Collection Container Corporation of America
200. **The Identification Manual** (open)
1964
Oil and assemblage on canvas, left panel: 32 x 25″
center panel: 72 x 52″
Collection Container Corporation of America
201. **The Second Greatest Homosexual** (discards)
1965
Oil and collage on paper, 24 x 15¾″
Collection Mr. and Mrs. Scott Hodes
Chicago, Illinois
202. **Six Flowers**
1965
Oil on board relief, 14½ x 16″
Private collection
203. **Lions on the Dreyfus Fund IV**
1964
Oil and collage, stencil cut-out on canvas, 60½ x 60½″
Private collection
204. **The History of the Russian Revolution from Marx to Mayakovsky** (detail)
1965
Mixed media construction, 53 pieces, 14′4″ x 32′5″ x 18″
The Hirshhorn Museum and Sculpture Garden
Washington, D.C.
205. **The Second Greatest Homosexual**
1965
Mixed media, 74½ x 62½″
Collection the artist
206. **Tinguely (Storm Window)**
1965
Oil and collage on board with storm window
29 x 25 x x 23¾″
Collection the artist
207. **Portrait of Herbert Lee**
1965
Relief, mixed media, 74½ x 54 x 13″
Collection Mr. and Mrs. Herbert C. Lee
Belmont, Massachusetts
208. **French Bank Note**
1961-65
Oil on canvas, 34 x 54½ x 5″
Private collection
209. **Don't Fall and Me**
1966
Oil and collage on canvas mounted on wood
16¼ x 28″
Collection the artist
210. **Advertisement for Helene Spitzer**
1966
Oil and collage on canvas, 58 x 59½ x 3″
Collection Mrs. Helene Spitzer, New York
211. **Study for "Lamp Man Loves It"**
1966
Plastic and painted wood mounted on wood box with electric light, 29¾ x 24 x 3⅝″
Collection the artist
212. **Don't Fall**
1966
Electric construction, 34¼ x 24 x 8½″
Collection the artist
213. **Webster and Cigars**
1966
Mixed media, collage on wood construction
13¼ x 16 x 13¼″
Collection the artist
214. **In Memory of the Dead**
1967
Spray paint and collage in relief, 30 x 21″
Collection the artist
215. **Covering the Earth**
1967
Mixed media, 48 x 37½ x 18″
Marlborough Gallery, New York
216. **Throwaway Dress: New York to Nairobi**
1967
Oil on canvas and wood construction, 45¾ x 78 x 3″
Marlborough Gallery, New York
217. **Cropped Blue Bed**
1967
Mixed media, 47½ x 48 x 40¾″
Collection the artist
218. **Shrimpton's Vinyl**
1969
Vinyl and collage, 33″ high
Private collection
219. **Norman Mailer: Study for Time Magazine Cover**
1968
Collage relief, 11½ x 8½″
Collection the artist
220. **Me and My Shadow I**
1970
Canvas, photomontage, plastic,
wood, plexiglas
79 x 71½ x 24½″
Collection the artist
221. **Me and My Shadow IV**
1970
Canvas, photomontage, plastic, wood
78¼ x 74 x 31¼″
Collection the artist
222. **Bad Witch**
1970
Mixed media, 90 x 64″
Collection the artist
223. **Wooden Dutch Masters**
1971
Wood encased in plastic, 10¾ x 16¼″
Private collection
224. **Miss Popcorn**
1972
Acrylic on vinyl, 72 x 43″
Museo de Arte Contemporáneo, Caracas, Venezuela

225. **Umber and Pink Jemima,**
Portrait of Hattie McDaniel
1973
Acrylic on vinyl, 32½ x 48½″
Private collection

226. **Movie House**
1973
Mixed media, air brush, 72¼ x 184¾ x 6″
Private collection

227. **Garbage**
1973
Mixed media collage on canvas, 90 x 90″
Butler Institute of American Art
Youngstown, Ohio
Gift of Professor and Mrs. Sam Hunter

228. **Portrait of Miss Oregon II**
1973
Acrylic on canvas, 66 x 108″
Private collection

229. **Beauty and Beast I**
1975
Acrylic on canvas, 114 x 60″
Collection Sivia and Jeffrey H. Loria, New York

230. **The Stripe is in the Eye of the Beholder**
1975
Acrylic on canvas, 85¾ x 100½″
Private collection

231. **The Continuing Interest in Abstract Art:**
Happy Frank, No. 2
1981
Pencil on paper mounted on canvas, 28¾ x 42″
Collection the artist

232. **Chinese Information (Travel I)**
1980
Oil on canvas, 120 x 144″
Private collection

233. **Chinese. Information (Travel II)**
1980
Oil on canvas, 120 x 144″
Private collection

DRAWINGS

234. **Portrait of Jane Freilicher**
1950
Pencil on paper, 13½ x 10⅞″
Collection the artist

235. **Rabbi Reading, Study for "The Burial"**
1951
Charcoal, 16½ x 14″
Collection the artist

236. **From Rembrandt**
1952
Pencil, 16½ x 13¾″
Collection the artist

237. **Study for "The Burial"**
1951
Charcoal, 14 x 16½″
Collection the artist

238. **Bathers (after Cézanne)**
1952
Pastel and pencil, 13¾ x 16½″
Collection Mr. and Mrs. George L. Sturman
Chicago, Illinois

239. **After David**
1952
Pencil on paper, 14 x 14″
Collection the artist

240. **Study for "Washington Crossing the Delaware"**
1953
Pencil, 11 x 13⅝″
Museum of Modern Art, New York

241. **Study for "Washington Crossing the Delaware"**
(two heads and a horse)
1953
Pencil, 11 x 13⅝″
Museum of Modern Art, New York

242. **George Washington**
1953
Pencil and collage, 13⅞ x 15⅝″
Menil Foundation Collection, Houston, Texas

243. **Portrait of John Ashbery**
1953
Pastel, 13¾ x 16¼″
Museum of Modern Art, New York

244. **Portrait of Kenneth Koch**
1953
Pencil, 13¾ x 16¾″
Museum of Modern Art, New York

245. **Frank O'Hara**
1953
Pencil on paper, 6⅛ x 5⅛″
Museum of Modern Art, New York

246. **Portrait of Augusta**
1953
Pencil on paper, 14 x 11″
Collection of the artist

247. **Augusta**
1953
Pencil on paper, 14 x 11″
Collection the artist

248. **Robertus**
1954
Pencil heightened with white gouache, 12 x 14¼″
Collection the artist

249. **Edwin Denby**
1953
Pencil on paper, 16⅝ x 19¾″
Museum of Modern Art, New York

250. **Joseph Seated**
1954
Pencil on paper, 11 x 14″
Collection Ellen Adler, New York

251. **Frank O'Hara with Boots on Study for "O'Hara"**
1954
Pencil on paper, 24¾ x 18¾″
Collection the artist

252. **Berdie Seated on Bed**
1954
Pencil on paper, 18¾ x 24⅞″
Collection the artist

253. **Sonia, the Artist's Mother**
1954
Pencil on paper, 16⅝ x 13¾″
Collection the artist

254. **Portrait of Grace Hartigan**
1954
Pencil on paper, 25 x 18″
Collection Jane Freilicher, New York

255. **Flower Studies after Leonardo** (detail)
1954
Pencil, 13¾ x 16½" (full size)
Collection the artist

256. **Middle Europe, Double Portrait of Myself**
1954
Pencil on paper, 18½ x 24¼"
Private collection

257. **Joan Mitchel in a Summer Hat**
1955
Pencil on paper, 13⅞ x 16½"
Collection Richard and Carol Selle
Chicago, Illinois

258. **Head of Joseph**
1956
Pencil, 12 x 9"
Collection the artist

259. **Brushes and Cooper's Hawk**
1956
Pencil on paper, 14 x 16½"
Private collection

260. **Moustache Portrait of Pierre Restenay**
1956
Pencil on paper, 14 x 15"
Collection the artist

261. **Child with Dolls**
1956
Pencil, 16½ x 13"
Collection the artist

262. **Frank O'Hara Seated with Hands Clasped**
1956
Pencil on paper, 18 x 14½"
Collection the artist

263. **John Myers**
1957
Pencil on paper, 14 x 16⅞"
Collection the artist

264. **Female Karl Marx**
1959
Pencil on paper, 13⅞ x 16½"
Collection the artist

265. **Stones: US,** collaboration with Frank O'Hara
1958
Lithograph, 24 x 30"
Collection the artist

266. **Rejected Copy**
1978
Pencil and colored paper on paper, 24 x 20"
Private collection

267. **The Continuing Interest in Abstract Art:
Emma and Dad**
1981
Pencil and colored pencil on paper, 27½ x 32"
Collection the artist

268. **Stephen (14th Birthday)**
1959
Pencil on paper, 13 x 15"
Collection the artist

269. **Gregory Corso as an Electric Fan**
1959
Pencil, 14 x 17"
Collection the artist

270. **Record Cover for Jack Teagarden**
1960
Pencil and collage on paper, 13⅞ x 13¾"
Columbia Records, New York

271. **Drawing for Kerouac-Beat**
1960
Pencil, 16½ x 13⅜"
Collection Rotrot Klein Moquit, Phoenix, Arizona

272. **The Last Civil War Veteran**
1961
Pencil on paper with collage heightened with
white gouache, 10 x 8"
Thomas E. Benesch Memorial Collection
Museum of Art, Baltimore, Maryland

273. **Clarice: Crossed Ankles**
1961
Pencil on paper, 11½ x 9"
Private collection

274. **Small Friendship of America and France**
1961
Pencil on paper, 9 x 10½"
Private collection

275. **How to Draw Reclining Nudes and
Rectangles with Legs**
1962
Collage and watercolor, 14 x 17"
Private collection

276. **How to Draw Noses**
1962
Watercolor, pencil and collage, 14⅝ x 12½"
Formerly collection James Thrall Soby
New Canaan, Connecticut

277. **Camels**
1961
Pencil on paper, 17 x 14"
Private collection

278. **Study for Second Version of George Washington
Crossing the Delaware,**
1960
Pencil, 19⅞ x 26⅛"
Museum of Modern Art, New York

279. **Transit**
1961
Pencil and collage, 13⅜ x 16⅜"
Private collection

280. **How to Draw Series: Oreilles [Ears]**
1962
Collage with gouache, pencil, charcoal,
photomechanical reproduction, and cellophane
tape on paper, 9¼ x 10⅜"
The Hirshhorn Museum and Sculpture Garden
Washington, D.C.

281. **How to Draw Series: Pieds [Feet]**
1962
Collage with gouache, pencil, charcoal,
photomechanical reproduction, and cellophane
tape on paper, 14⅜ x 10½"
The Hirshhorn Museum and Sculpture Garden
Washington, D.C.

282. **Camels**
1962
Pencil on paper, 14½ x 13"
Private collection

283. **Portrait of Mary McCarthy**
1962
Pencil on paper, 14½ x 16¼"
Collection Mr. and Mrs. Stanley S. Arkin, New York

284. **How to Draw Series: Visage**
1963
Collage with pencil and charcoal on paper, 9¼ x 10⅜"
The Hirshhorn Museum and Sculpture Garden
Washington, D.C.

285. **Grey Webster**
1963
Pencil and crayon on paper, 9 x 9⅛"
Private collection

286. **Anemones**
1963
Pencil and colored papers on board, 9 x 10"
Collection Clarice Rivers, New York

287. **Bank Note**
1962
Pencil, 15¼ x 18½"
Collection Mr. and Mrs. Leonard Kasle
Franklin, Michigan

288. **French Postage Stamps**
1963
Pencil and collage, 10 x 9½"
Collection the artist

289. **De Kooning Drawing II**
1963
Pencil drawing, 13½ x 11½"
Collection Lester Avnet, New York

290. **Portrait of Imamu Baraka as Le Roi Jones**
1963
Pencil on paper, 14 x 16¾"
Private collection

291. **Portrait of Ornette Coleman, Illustration of Firbank's New Rhythm—Auto**
1962
Pencil and collage on paper, 14 x 16½"
Collection the artist

292. **Papa a Little Later**
1964
Pencil on paper, 18 x 18"
Collection Mr. and Mrs. Edward S. Gordon
New York

293. **Mama a Little Later**
1964
Pencil on paper, 18 x 18"
Collection Mr. and Mrs. Edward S. Gordon
New York

294. **Portrait of Le Roi Jones, Study for Poster for Two One-Act Plays The Toilet and The Slave**
1964
Crayon and photograph on board, relief, 15 x 12"
Private collection

295. **Negative Lion**
1964
Pencil, crayon and collage, 19 x 14¼"
Private collection

296. **Lions on Dreyfus Fund**
1964
Pencil, collage, and crayon, 17¼ x 23¼"
Private collection

297. **Head of Leonard Bernstein**
1965
Pencil on music paper, 14 x 16"
Collection Leonard Bernstein

298. **John Lindsay Collage**
1965
Pencil and crayon on board collage, 23½ x 22½"
Collection John M. Rodger, Jr., Cleveland, Ohio

299. **Template, Horse, Butterflies and Birds**
1965
Mixed media with collage on wood, 14⅛ x 18"
Private collection

300. **Crows**
1965
Oil, crayon and pencil on board, 14⅛ x 16¾"
Collection the artist

301. **Stravinsky Collage**
1966
Collage with pencil, pastel and crayon, 12⅜ x 25½"
Svensk-Franska Konstgalleret, Stockholm, Sweden

302. **Drawing for Lamp Man Loves It**
Pencil, oil and collage on paper, 57¾ x 47"
Collection the artist

303. **Portrait of Sam Hunter**
1965
Pencil on graph paper, 14 x 18"
Private collection

304. **Elimination of Nostalgia I**
1967
Crayon and pencil relief on board, 12 x 9¼"
Collection Mr. and Mrs. Marco de Laurenti, New York

305. **Congolese Woman and Lion**
1968
Pencil and collage, 24 x 18"
Private collection

306. **Janet Seated**
1968
Pencil, ballpoint, day-glo paper and collage, 18 x 24"
Private collection

307. **Dutch Masters Silver**
1968
Construction with pencil, crayon, silverpaper
11¾ x 16 x 8¼"
Private collection

308. **Black is Black**
1968
Mixed media on pink pinstripe paper, 25⅜ x 20"
Private collection

309. **Snow Cap**
1970
Paper collage with pencil and colored crayon
encased in plastic, 17 x 14"
Private collection

310. **Study for the Boston Massacre I**
1970
Colored pencil on posterboard, 32 x 40"
Private collection

311. **Tryout for Boston Massacre** (three soldiers, one mounted, with banners)
1970
Colored pencil on posterboard, 32 x 40"
Collection the artist

312. **Portrait of Aladar as a Hollow Column**
1971
Pencil and tape on paper in plastic, 14 x 16"
Collection Aladar Marberger, New York

313. **Self Portrait**
1972
Pencil with poloroid photograph, 39½ x 50"
Collection Earl McGrath, Los Angeles, California

314. **Study after the Boston Massacre III**
1970
Colored pencil and cutout on posterboard, 40 x 32"
Collection the artist

315. **Mr. Steel (Leonard Kasle)**
1971
Collage encased in red plastic, 14 x 17"
Collection Mr. and Mrs. Leonard Kasle
Franklin, Michigan

316. **Dutch Master VF**
1971
Paper collage with charcoal and colored pencil,
encased in plastic, 9¼ x 14¾"
Private collection

317. **Kinko and the Carp**
1974
Pencil on paper, 40 x 56"
Private collection

318. **Portrait of Miss Oregon I**
1973
Mixed media on paper, 66 x 108"
Collection Leonard Holzer, New York

319. **Utamaro's Courtesans**
1974
Pencil and colored pencil on paper, 81½ x 70"
Collection Killy Myers, New York

320. **Working Drawing for "Shushui's Erotic Art"**
1974
Pencil and colored pencil on tracing paper, 54 x 80¼"
Private collection

321. **Working Drawing of Hero for
"Heroes of Chushingura"**
1974
Pencil and colored pencil on tracing paper
80½ x 54"
Private collection

322. **For C's 35th**
1974
Colored pencil on paper, 14 x 17"
Collection Clarice Rivers, New York

323. **Portrait of Sheila**
1975
Pencil on paper
Private collection

324. **Homage to Picasso**
1974
Pencil, photograph collage, 22 x 30¼"
Collection the artist

325. **The Stripe is in the Eye of the Beholder:
Portrait of Barnett Newman**
1975
Pencil on paper, 35¾ x 100½"
Collection Mr. David Pincus, New York

326. **Joe Glazer Sings Garbage**
1977
Collage with pencil, 18¼ x 18⅛"
Private collection

327. **Two Lines of the Depression**
1975
Pencil and colored pencil on paper, 84 x 84"
Marlborough Gallery, New York

328. **Nigeria Yesterday and Today Carbon Color**
1976
Pencil and carbon paper, 25½ x 40"
Private collection

329. **Burundi Stamps Carbon Color**
1976
Pencil and carbon paper, 25⅝ x 36⅝"
Collection the artist

330. **French Camel Carbon Color**
1976
Pencil and carbon paper, 36 x 46½"
Private collection

331. **Discontinued French Money**
1976
Pencil on paper collage, 27¼ x 37¾"
Collection the artist

332. **Gwynne and Emma Rivers, Carbon Drawing**
1976
Colored carbon on paper, 23½ x 33¾"
Collection Susan Lloyd, Paris

333. **Reclining Figure**
1977
Pencil on paper, 10¾ x 14¾"
Private collection

334. **Scale Drawing for Rainbow Rembrandt's**
1977
Pencil on colored carbon and paper, 65 x 75½"
The Hirshhorn Museum and Sculpture Garden
Washington, D.C.

335. **Two Camels**
1978
Pencil and colored pencil on acetate, 15 x 21½"
Private collection

336. **Webster**
1978
Pencil, colored pencil and acrylic on paper, 26 x 30½"
Private collection

337. **Golden Oldies: Camels**
1978
Pencil and pastel on paper, 64 x 54"
Collection Ron Seff, New York

338. **Ace of Spades**
1978
Black pencil on acetate, 27½ x 24"
Private collection

339. **Pair of Kings**
1978
Pencil and colored pencil on paper, 24½ x 25"
Private collection

340. **Dying and Dead Veteran**
1978
Acrylic and charcoal on paper, 71 x 59"
Private collection

341. **Polish Vocabulary Lesson**
1978
Acrylic, pencil and colored pencil on paper, 18½ x 13¾"
Private collection

342. **Italian Vocabulary Lesson**
1978
Pencil and colored pencil on paper, 17½ x 14"
Private collection

343. **Study for "Chinese Information-Travel"**
1980
Charcoal, colored pencil and collage on paper
30¼ x 35¼"
Collection the artist

344. **Go Go and Camels**
1978
Colored pencil and acrylic on canvas, 60 x 40"
Private collection

345. **The Continuing Interest in Abstract Art: Graduation**
1981
Pencil on paper mounted on canvas, 25½ x 34″
Collection the artist

346. **Webster on Hand-Made Paper**
1979
Pencil and colored pencil on paper, 13¾ x 17″
Private collection

347. **Posing (Henry Geldzahler)**
1981
Pencil and colored pencil on paper, 23½ x 28″
Private collection

348. **The Continuing Interest in Abstract Art: Frank and Susan in 1967**
1981
Relief, 39⅞ x 31⅛″
Collection the artist

349. **In the Artist's Studio Vertical**
1981
Pencil, colored pencil and tape on paper, 33⅜ x 23½″
Private collection

350. **Portrait of Mayor Koch**
1985
Pencil on paper
Private collection

351. **For the Magician of Lublin**
1983
Pencil and colored pencil mounted on canvas
17¼ x 19⅝″
Collection the artist

352. **Primo Levi: Witness Drawing**
1988
Pencil and pastel on paper, 26½ x 28½″
Collection the artist

PHOTOGRAPH CREDITS:

We wish to express our gratitude to all those people and bodies who have lent us photographs or have authorized us to reproduce works from their collections in this book.

Aida and Bob Mates
Rudolph Burckhardt
Geoffrey Clements, New York
Jonas Dovydenas
Susan Einstein, Santa Monica
Peter A. Juley & Son, New York
Robert E. Mates
Robert E. Mates and Paul Katz
Robert E. Mates and Gail Stern
Peter Moore, New York
Otto E. Nelson, New York
Edward Oleksak
Ellen Page Wilson, New York
Eric Pollitzer, New York
Nathan Rabin, New York
John Reed
Tony Rogers
Noel Rowe
Ken Showell, New York
Steven Sloman, New York
Adolph Studly, New York
John Tennant
John F. Waggaman, New York